THE PITTSBURGH CRAWFORDS
The Lives and Times of Black Baseball's Most Exciting Team

THE PITTSBURGH CRAWFORDS

The Lives and Times of Black Baseball's Most Exciting Team

James Bankes

Cover design by Andy Nelson

Cover photo from Refocus Productions

The credits section for this book begins on page 163, and is considered an extension of the copyright page.

Library of Congress Catalog Card Number: 90–83701

ISBN 0–697–12889–X

Printed in the United States of America by Wm. C. Brown Publishers, 2460 Kerper Boulevard, Dubuque, IA 52001

10 9 8 7 6 5 4 3 2 1

For Ham

A great baseball player and a cherished friend

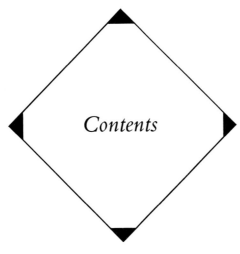

Contents

Ted Williams

Foreword

*A*merica promises every individual the opportunity to reach his or her full potential and I was very fortunate to have played in the major leagues. I had the chance to go as far as natural ability and hard work would carry me. I've often wondered what might have happened to me without baseball. A chill goes up my back when I think I might have been denied the opportunity to play in the major leagues if I had been black.

I was very pleased in 1972 when Satchel Paige, one of the old Negro League stars, was enshrined in the Baseball Hall of Fame. Satchel did have a brief major league career, but long after his prime. I hit against him in the American League when he was an old man, and he was still tough. I can imagine how good he was in his younger days.

Many of the other black stars never played in a major league game. Among the nine deserving negro league players who have entered the Hall, four of them, Josh Gibson, Cool Papa Bell, Oscar Charleston, and Judy Johnson, played with Satchel on the great Pittsburgh Crawfords club of the 1930s. What a group they must have been!

Other than Satchel, I didn't have the opportunity to play against any of the Crawfords or even see them play. So I'm very happy that Jim Bankes has told their story. I hope you enjoy his book and I also hope you'll learn something about life in black baseball.

Ted Williams

Preface

The Pittsburgh Crawfords may have been the greatest black baseball team of all time. They were certainly the most exciting. The heart of their lineup featured five men destined for Cooperstown's Hall of Fame: fireballing Satchel Paige, one of the very best pitchers in baseball history; slugging catcher Josh Gibson, who could hit the ball as far and as often as anybody, including Ruth of the Yankees; sleek center fielder Cool Papa Bell, the fastest runner the game has ever known; volatile first baseman Oscar Charleston, perhaps black baseball's best player; and the masterful third baseman, Judy Johnson. This awesome group, complemented by other stars, powered the Crawfords to the very zenith of black baseball and they did so with marvelous style and grace.

I've learned about the Pittsburgh Crawfords through extensive interviews with Paige, Bell, and Johnson, as well as speedsters Jimmie Crutchfield and Ted Page. I want to thank each of them for their help.

I also wish to thank the man I call Mr. Commissioner. Albert B. "Happy" Chandler, while baseball commissioner, stood with lonely courage to open the door for Jackie Robinson and the other blacks who followed him into the major leagues.

I commend Ted Williams for his eloquent comments about black baseball players during his Hall of Fame induction speech at Cooperstown in 1966. His words helped open the Great Hall for a number of worthy black men.

John Holway, black baseball's most eminent historian and researcher, must also be remembered. Primarily because of his efforts in compiling oral histories and statistics, black baseball has begun to emerge from the mist. Even more important, John's sincere interest has provided much happiness for many of the old black players during the final years of their lives.

The encouragement and genuine interest of Ed Bartell, my editor at Wm. C. Brown, has been inspirational. I hope someday we can play catch on the field of dreams.

Many thanks to my son, Paul. His research efforts have proven very valuable.

Now, please enjoy the vibrant electricity of the magnificent Pittsburgh Crawfords.

James Bankes
From the North Coast of Oregon
June 1, 1990

THE PITTSBURGH CRAWFORDS
The Lives and Times of Black Baseball's Most Exciting Team

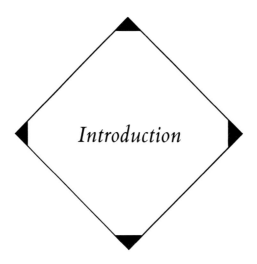

Introduction

I've known Jim Bankes for a long time, and I have no better friend. He's a man with big shoulders and those shoulders have carried me many places. We've traveled together to Cooperstown, to New York City, to the 50th Anniversary All-Star game in Chicago, to ball games here in St. Louis, and to the Negro League Reunion in Ashland, Kentucky.

Ashland was the first time Jim went with me, and I think he was a little nervous about meeting all of my friends. He was a newcomer, a young white man among old black men. So, when I introduced him to the guys, I just said to them, he's a pro. They all knew that meant two things. One, he knew baseball. Two, he could be trusted. He's never let me down either way.

Several times, when Jim has given speeches about me, I've cried. But they have been tears of joy because his words have been so beautiful. He cares about me and my family and my friends.

So, I'm very happy Jim is telling the story of the Pittsburgh Crawfords. I played on some great teams. One was the St. Louis Stars of the 1920s and another was the Homestead Grays of the 1940s. But the Crawfords were the best. In fact, I don't think there has ever been a better team than the Crawfords. We could have played with anybody. I just wish we had been given the chance.

For Satch, Josh, Judy, Ted, Charleston, Bankhead, and all the other Crawfords, I thank Jim Bankes for writing this book. I wish they all could have lived to read it.

Cool Papa Bell

3

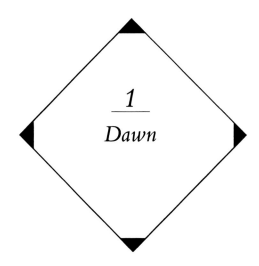

1

Dawn

Baseball is a legitimate profession. It should be taken seriously by the colored player. An honest effort of his great ability will open the avenue in the near future wherein he may walk hand in hand with the opposite race in the greatest of all American games—baseball.

Sol White, 1906
History of Colored Baseball

Sol White lived to see his dream come true when Jackie Robinson played his first game for the Brooklyn Dodgers in 1947. But from 1899 until Robinson's time, a gentleman's agreement among the white masters of baseball banned blacks from both the major and minor leagues. Only white men such as Ty Cobb, Rogers Hornsby, and Lefty Grove reaped the rewards of being national baseball heroes.

Some of the most gifted athletes who ever stepped on a diamond played behind this white curtain, both before and after 1899. Others, only journeyman ballplayers, just tried to survive and to earn a living in a land governed by Jim Crow. These courageous men pioneered the way for Jackie Robinson and for the great black teams, among them the Pittsburgh Crawfords.

Some of these pioneers integrated America's game before the door closed tight in 1899. Ironically, John "Bud" Fowler, hailed from Cooperstown, New York, the legendary home of Abner Doubleday's first baseball game. In 1872, just seven years after the close of the Civil War, and only three years after the Cincinnati Red Stockings established themselves as the first professional club, Fowler joined the white team in New Castle, Pennsylvania, becoming the first professional black player. Primarily a second baseman, he barnstormed across America for the next 25 years, and in 1887 he hit .350 and stole 30 bases for the Binghamton, New York, club.

Moses Fleetwood Walker, the next black player of significance, combined intellectual ability with athletic prowess. In 1878, at the age of 21, he entered Oberlin College in Ohio. During his final year at Oberlin in 1881, he became the catcher on the newly formed varsity baseball team. Oberlin played three games and won them all, including a victory over the University of Michigan.

Walker left Oberlin at the end of the year without earning a degree and enrolled at Michigan. He won varsity baseball letters there in 1882 and 1883.

After one season at Michigan, Walker left and returned to Ohio, where he joined the Toledo baseball club of the Northwestern League. Toledo won the pennant with Walker catching 60 games and posting a .251 batting average. The next season, he became the first black major leaguer when Toledo joined the two-year-old American Association, recognized as a major league along with the much older National League. Fleet Walker's mediocre career lasted through seven seasons of almost continuous racial abuse.

Frank Grant, perhaps the best of the black players before the turn of the century, began his career in 1886 with the Meriden, Connecticut, team of the Eastern League. He hit .325 at Meriden, but later in the season he moved to the Buffalo

Moses Fleetwood Walker—the first black
major leaguer.

Bisons of the International League and blistered the ball at a .340 clip. In 1887,
Grant led Buffalo to a second place finish with a .366 average and led the league
with 27 doubles, 10 triples, and 11 home runs. He also stole 40 bases.

Grant forged another outstanding season in 1888, with a .326 average, 19 doubles, 6 triples, 11 home runs, and 26 steals. Instead of furthering his career, however, success worked against him by calling attention to his color. The other Bison
players refused to let him sit with them for the official team photograph, while
opposition pitchers consistently threw at him and base runners coming into second
base made serious, and often successful, attempts to spike him.

Buffalo failed to offer Grant a contract for the 1899 season and he signed with
Harrisburg, Pennsylvania, of the Eastern League, where he played for three years.
From 1892, until the end of his career after the 1903 season, Grant never again
played for a white team.

Southpaw George Stovey, the first black pitcher, began his career in 1886 with Jersey City of the Eastern League, and in 1887, with Newark of the International League, he posted a brilliant mark of 33–14. During his magnificent season, Stovey became one of the central figures in an incident that led to the eventual exclusion of black players from organized white baseball. On July 19, Newark had scheduled an exhibition game against the National League's Chicago White Stockings, managed by Constantine "Cap" Anson, baseball's first real superstar. Stovey, being the ace of Newark's staff, drew the starting assignment against Chicago, but on the day of the game, he begged off because of illness.

Newark won the game anyway, but the circumstances of Stovey's absence emerged as a racial confrontation. Rather than being sick, Stovey had backed out because the popular and powerful Anson had refused to put his team on the field against a black man. Anson's action set the precedent that led to the banishment of blacks from white baseball by 1899.

Sol White, a middle infielder of exceptional ability, often hit in the high .300s, and had a brilliant career before the turn of the century. But White's greatest contribution lay in keeping alive the dream of integrated baseball. In 1902, Walter Schlichter, sports editor of the white *Philadelphia Item,* decided to put together a new black team. He called his club the Philadelphia Giants and hired Sol White to be his manager. White immediately recruited Frank Grant, along with third baseman Bill Monroe and outfielder Andrew "Jap" Payne, to form the nucleus of the team. A number of black teams had emerged by this time, most notably the powerful Cuban Giants, but this group was special. They rolled to an 81–43 record and claimed the Eastern Black Championship.

Schlichter and White even decided to challenge the Philadelphia Athletics, champions of the American League, to a short exhibition series. The Athletics had enough to win both games, 8–3 and 13–9, but manager White slammed three hits in the second contest.

In 1906, White penned his poignant tribute to the courageous black pioneers, *History of Colored Baseball.* At the same time, he continued his struggle to keep the Giants going in the face of severe financial problems. The team folded in 1911, but Sol White remained one of the most respected men in black baseball until his death, just one year after the game became integrated once more.

Another astute baseball man also dreamed of integrating baseball. He was John McGraw, the fierce competitor who in 1901 managed the Baltimore Orioles of the new American League. That March, during spring training in Hot Springs, Arkansas, McGraw became quite interested in the play of some of the bellboys at the Eastland Hotel. One of them, Charles Grant, had played second base for the

John Henry Lloyd

black Columbia Giants of Chicago in 1901. McGraw decided the young man had enough ability to play in the major leagues. But how could he overcome the color barrier?

McGraw's inspiration came from a map, where he noticed Tokohoma Creek. He named Grant "Chief Tokohoma" and said he was a Cherokee Indian. Predictably, the disguise failed and Grant never played a regular season game for Baltimore.

Even as Sol White's Philadelphia Giants suffered their demise, New York City began to emerge as the heart of Eastern black baseball. From Harlem came the

Lincoln Giants, formerly of Lincoln, Nebraska, one of the best teams in baseball history, black or white. The Lincolns, like the Pittsburgh Crawfords, were loaded with talent. Smokey Joe Williams and Cannonball Dick Redding headed the pitching staff, complemented by catcher Louis Santop, shortstop John Henry Lloyd, and center fielder Spotswood Poles. Lloyd's plaque resides in the Hall of Fame. The others should be there too.

Texan Joe Williams joined the Lincoln Giants in 1912 and spent 12 seasons with them. At 6'5", he often intimidated batters, buggywhipping his fastball and cracking his curve with a big overhand motion. Williams joined the Giants at age 26, the very prime of his career, and dominated all opposition. His victims included an impressive array of major league teams. During 1912, for instance, he shutout the New York Giants twice, 2–0 and 6–0. He also whitewashed the New York Highlanders 6–0.

Williams really warmed up in 1913. Although losing to an All-Star contingent, 1–0, he fanned 13. He later beat the same group 7–3, with 14 strikeouts. He then went up against the Philadelphia Phillies and their ace right-hander, Grover Cleveland Alexander. Alexander, with 373 career victories, ranks as one of the greatest pitchers in history. On this day, however, Williams bested him 9–2. Smokey Joe also beat another future resident of Cooperstown, Chief Bender, 2–1.

In 1914, Williams beat the Phillies 10–4, and then hooked up in a monumental duel with Rube Marquard of the New York Giants, another future Hall-of-Famer. The game ended in a 1–1 tie, as each man allowed just three hits. Marquard whiffed 14, and Williams 12.

Big Joe had a bad year against major leaguers in 1915, winning 1 and losing 2. He didn't pitch against any big league teams in 1916, but 1917 was a different story. Williams began with a 10-inning no-hitter and 20 strikeouts against the New York Giants, champions of the National League. Unfortunately, he lost 1–0. Smokey Joe also beat Bender again, 11–1, and outpitched the great Walter Johnson, 1–0.

Williams won three games against big leaguers in 1918, including another victory over Marquard, and on opening day in 1919, he pitched what he called the greatest game of his life. This time the competition was black and the opposing pitcher was his old teammate on the Lincoln Giants, Cannonball Dick Redding. Williams won it 1–0, pitching another no-hitter. Redding allowed only two hits.

From 1912 to 1914, Williams teamed with Dick Redding to give the Lincoln Giants one of the best pitching combinations in history. Another big man at 6'4", Redding earned his nickname of "Cannonball" because of the enormous velocity of his fastball. He was frightening on the mound, turning his back to the hitter during his windup, much in the same fashion as Satchel Paige did with his famous hesitation pitch. Dick also showed little reluctance in buzzing any man who dug in too aggressively or tried to take away the plate.

Redding's career began in 1910 with Sol White's Philadelphia Giants. During spring training in 1911, he pitched batting practice for the New York Giants and made a big impression on manager John McGraw with his speed. After failing with Charles Grant, McGraw encouraged Redding to move to New York, hoping he might be the one to break the color barrier.

Once in New York, Dick joined the Lincoln Giants and won 17 straight games, including several no-hitters. Redding had another excellent year in 1912, but in 1913 he shifted into high gear. He won 43 and lost only 12, including a perfect game against Jersey City of the Eastern League. In another game he fanned 24, and in yet another, he pitched six innings, striking out 15 of the 18 batters who braved his cannonball.

Over the years, Redding pitched very well against big league competition, but only a few of his performances have been preserved. In 1918, however, he went up against Carl Mays, the submarine pitcher of the Boston Red Sox, who would kill shortstop Ray Chapman of the Cleveland Indians the following season by hitting him in the head with a pitch. Redding lost a 14-inning confrontation with Mays 2–1. He also lost in 1918 to big Jeff Tesreau of the New York Giants, again by a score of 2–1.

In addition to the pitching brilliance of Williams and Redding, the Giants also had plenty of offensive firepower. Their fleet lead off man, Spotswood Poles, played a splendid center field and swung the bat with authority. In 1911, for example, he hit .440 with 41 stolen bases. Poles found easy pickings against big league pitchers, hitting .610 against them between 1913 and 1917. Like Cool Papa Bell many years later, he was compared to Ty Cobb.

The Lincoln Giants' catcher, Louis Santop, hit from the left side with enormous power. He sometimes called his shot, as Babe Ruth possibly did in the third game of the 1932 World Series. On October 12, 1920, when the two great sluggers played against each other, Ruth went hitless, while Santop went three for four.

Santop played with the Lincoln Giants during their real glory years, hitting .470 in 1911, .422 in 1912, and .455 in 1914. The battery of Santop at 6'4", combined with either Joe Williams or Dick Redding, might well rank as the most physically intimidating combination in baseball history.

Even among all these great stars, shortstop John Henry Lloyd stood as the heart and soul of the Lincoln Giants. Lloyd was called the Black Wagner, a comparison to Honus Wagner of the Pittsburgh Pirates, who is considered the best shortstop ever and perhaps the best player ever. When told of the comparison, Wagner said, "I am honored to have John Lloyd called the Black Wagner. It is an honor to be compared with him."

Once during an interview, Babe Ruth was asked who he thought was the greatest player of all time. "You mean in the major leagues," replied Ruth. "No," came the response, "the greatest player anywhere." "Then," said Ruth, "I'd pick John Henry Lloyd."

In 1911, Lloyd joined the Lincoln Giants who were managed for the first half of the season by Sol White. When White left, Lloyd, the team captain, became manager. Under his leadership, the team rolled to victory after victory over both black and white opposition. One of their best years was 1913, with 101 victories and only 6 defeats.

Besides leadership, Lloyd provided superb defense and a big bat. He hit .475 in 1911 and .375 in 1912; and in the Lincolns' 1913 victory over the Philadelphia Phillies, he ripped Grover Cleveland Alexander for two hits and also stole four bases.

Lloyd's greatest success against major leaguers came in Cuba during the winter, when he played for the Havana Reds. In 1909, the Reds played an 11-game series against the Detroit Tigers and won seven. Eustaquio Pedroso even pitched a 10-inning no-hitter against the American Leaguers. Lloyd hit .546 for the season against big league pitching, including several hits off Addie Joss and Mordecai "Three Finger" Brown, both future Hall-of-Famers.

In 1909, Tiger slugger Ty Cobb had missed the trip to Cuba. He went for revenge in 1910. The Georgia Peach hit well as the Tigers won four of the five games he played.

Cobb, with sharpened spikes glistening, also wanted to show the black upstarts how he ran the bases. Lloyd prepared for his attack by wearing cast-iron shin guards under his baseball stockings. Poor Tyrus never really had a chance. Besides John Henry's surprise, Cobb faced the rifle arm of black catcher Bruce Petway. He tried to steal twice and was thrown out both times. On his third try, he was out by such a wide margin that he just turned around and ran off the field, snarling and cursing. Cobb vowed never to play against blacks again, and he never did.

Lloyd hit .500 for the series. He was followed by another American black, Grant "Home Run" Johnson, who hit .412, and by Petway who hit .388. Cobb finished fourth at .369 and his teammate Sam Crawford posted a .360 average.

Connie Mack's Philadelphia Athletics, fresh from trouncing the Chicago Cubs in the World Series, followed the Tigers into Havana. The Reds swept three games as Lloyd hit .300 against Chief Bender and Gettysburg Eddie Plank, two more Hall of Fame hurlers.

John Henry Lloyd's Lincoln Giants were by no means the only great team during the early years of black baseball. Sol White's Philadelphia Giants must be considered, as well as C. I. Taylor's Indianapolis ABCs. In Chicago, the Leland Giants, later the Chicago American Giants, became a powerhouse under the direction of a genius named Rube Foster, who in time would be called The Father of Black Baseball.

2
Darling Rube

*Rube Foster was a great pitcher, a wonderful
manager, a team owner, and a league president.
How can a man do any more? He should have been
the first of the Blacks to go into the Hall of Fame.
I'm just glad he's there now. He was the Father of
Black Baseball you know.*

Cool Papa Bell, 1981
Cooperstown, New York

*T*he enshrinement of Andrew "Rube" Foster in the Baseball Hall of Fame in 1981 proves that if you wait long enough, justice prevails. Nine years after Satchel Paige was elected, Foster assumed his rightful position in the Great Hall. As Cool Papa says, he should have been the first. He was truly the Father of Black Baseball and one of the most influential figures in baseball history, black or white.

Foster in his various baseball endeavors established a tradition of class and style which Gus Greenlee followed when operating the Pittsburgh Crawfords. Within the obvious constraints of money and racism, Foster provided the best possible accommodations, transportation, uniforms, and equipment for his team. Greenlee did the same. The two men differed, however, in their standards for paying players. Foster was generous, while Greenlee was tight.

Both Foster and Greenlee realized that their players were highly visible in the black community. Therefore, even though a gangster himself, Greenlee carried on Foster's tradition of demanding that his players lead exemplary personal lives. Furthermore, the Crawfords' manager, Oscar Charleston, greatly admired Foster. Charleston's style of managing reflected Foster's emphasis on speed, precision, and strategy, rather than on sheer power.

Andrew Foster, destined for greatness, was born in Calvert, Texas, on September 17, 1879. His mother died when he was fourteen years old, and when his father remarried, he ran away to Fort Worth to seek his future in baseball. By the age of seventeen, he had established himself as the pitching mainstay of the barnstorming Waco Yellow Jackets and often pitched practice for major league clubs during their spring training sessions in Texas.

In 1902, and by then a full-grown man at 6'4" and 220 pounds, Foster pitched for the Cuban Giants of Philadelphia and earned his nickname of "Rube" when he defeated the Philadelphia Athletics' ace left-hander Rube Waddell, 5–2. The eccentric Waddell was 25–7 that year, but Foster may well have been the best pitcher in America with 51 victories.

One of the key pitches in Foster's repertoire was the screwball, and in the spring of 1903, wise John McGraw hired him to teach Christy Mathewson and Iron Man Joe McGinnity how to throw it. Foster's tutoring seemed to work wonders.

Mathewson, calling his new pitch the fadeaway, jumped from 14 wins in 1902 to 34 in 1903. McGinnity, who had won 29 games in 1900, and then fallen to just eight in 1902, rebounded with 30 victories.

Rube Foster

Foster moved to the Cuban X-Giants, also a Philadelphia club, for the 1903 season. That fall, the X-Giants challenged Sol White's Philadelphia Giants to a championship series. Foster dominated with his right arm and with his big bat. He pitched the opener, batted cleanup, and came away with a 3–1 win, allowing only three hits. White's club won the second game, but Foster came back to win the third 12–3, while contributing three hits of his own. The X-Giants won the series five games to two, with Foster earning four of the five victories.

Rube jumped to the Philadelphia Giants in 1904 and faced his old teammates in the fall World Series. He won the opener, 5–4, while fanning 18. He then clinched the series in the third game, 4–2, while allowing only two hits.

Foster moved to Chicago in 1909 to become the playing manager of Frank Leland's Giants. The Lelands responded by winning 110 games, 48 of them in a row, while losing only 10. Despite two more successful seasons, however, Foster fell out with Leland and began looking for greener grass.

Rube found the new grass with John Schorling, a white tavern operator, and brother-in-law of White Sox owner Charles Comiskey. When the White Sox moved to Comiskey Park in 1910, Schorling purchased South Side Park from the club. In 1911, he and Foster founded the Chicago American Giants, soon to become one of the great teams in black baseball history. In their inaugural season, the Giants won 123 and lost only 6. A ticket cost just 50 cents and included ice water, so Foster's dashing men often outdrew the Cubs and the White Sox.

Foster, the great pitcher and brilliant manager, was also a charmer. The fans loved him and he soon became one of Chicago's most popular personalities. Beaming his big beautiful smile, he called almost everyone "darling," even his close friends, the gruff Mr. John McGraw and heavyweight champion Jack Johnson. A former first baseman, Johnson had been Rube's teammate on the Philadelphia Giants in 1903 and 1904, before knocking out Tommy Burns for the championship in 1908. The champ often made promotional appearances when the American Giants played at home.

In 1913, with the law after him, Johnson turned to Foster for help. Under the conditions of the Mann Act, Judge George Carpenter had fined Johnson $1,000 and had sentenced him to one year in the Joliet Penitentiary for transporting a minor over state lines for sexual purposes. While free on bail, Johnson masqueraded as a baseball player and left Chicago on a train with the American Giants who were beginning a barnstorming trip to Canada. Once in Canada, he purchased tickets on the steamer Corinthia, bound for Paris. "It was easy," Johnson said later. "I just put a bag of bats on my shoulder and walked right past the cops."

Even as his playing days diminished and ended in 1915, Foster remained an imposing figure on the Chicago bench, continuing to draw fans with the sheer vibrance of his personality. They came to watch him as much as they did to see the game. He always put on a good show, giving signs with his pipe and with nods of his head. "He seemed so casual," says Cool Papa Bell. "You'd think you had his signs, and then the next day they would be completely different. He was such a smart man."

The stylish and talented American Giants traveled the country in private Pullman cars and thrashed most of their opposition, black and white. Foster guided the team with unsurpassed brilliance. Submarine pitcher Webster McDonald, an astute baseball man, played for Foster. Sitting on the long cool veranda of the Otesaga Hotel in Cooperstown, New York, on the day of Foster's Hall of Fame induction, he discussed the great man's leadership.

"First of all," he said, "Rube was a strict disciplinarian. There was no question he was the boss. You did it his way or you didn't play for him.

"When you were pitching, he called everything. I mean everything, what to pitch, where to pitch it, and even what motion to use. The catcher would give signs, but it didn't mean nothing. Your natural tendency was to resist so much authority, but you had no choice. Besides, he was right most of the time.

"Our catcher, Jim Brown, got into it with Rube once. Brown was kind of an ornery guy anyway. He came out to the mound to give me hell about a pitch I'd thrown. I told him Rube had called it. Well, Brown complained about Rube in a real loud voice. After the inning was over, Rube told Jim to go in the clubhouse and take off his uniform. Rube followed him in and locked the door. Brown was a big strong guy, but Rube just whipped him. Boy, was Rube tough!

"Now, in black baseball, the teams didn't have a lot of pitching depth. If you could get into the other guy's bullpen, you could usually win the game. In fact, I think the lack of pitching depth was the only real difference between our teams and major league teams.

"Anyway, when we went up against a veteran pitcher who couldn't be rattled, Rube's strategy was to wear him down. He was very definite about hitting only good pitches, and sometimes the batters weren't allowed to swing until they had two strikes. We also bunted to both sides of the mound to make the pitcher work even more. I've even seen Rube give the opposing pitcher an intentional pass just so he would have to run the bases. By the seventh inning, the American Giants were usually ready to move in for the kill.

"When we were on the mound, Rube didn't want us to strike everybody out. He wanted us to get the batters to hit the ball so we could save energy. He told us that strikeouts impressed the fans, but smart pitchers didn't worry about such things."

Foster wanted Cool Papa Bell very much for the American Giants and offered St. Louis several players for him in 1922. "I wish I could have played for him," Bell says. "His game was speed and so was mine.

"Don't get me wrong, I think Foster was the greatest man in black baseball, and he was very good to me, but I didn't approve of some of his methods. It's just like when people ask me who was the best between Joe Williams and Satchel Paige. I always say Paige, because Joe Williams cut the ball, and that's cheating.

"Before a home game, Foster would freeze the balls that were going to be pitched against the opposition. One of those big strong guys would come up and really connect. The ball would take off and then die like it had lead in it.

"He would also wet down the infield so much that it seemed like the middle of a rainstorm. Bunts would roll dead about 10 feet from home plate. He also built little ridges along the baselines. You could hardly see them, but they kept bunts from going foul.

"His favorite play was the steal and bunt. The runner on first would take off and the batter would bunt the ball so the third baseman had to field it. If he threw to first, the lead runner just kept going to third. If he held the ball, it was runners on first and second. It was a beautiful play and Foster's team made it work over and over again. To make it work, his guys had to be able to really place their bunts. They used to practice for hours bunting the ball into areas Rube would mark off with chalk.

"As it was, I tried to use his tricks against him. I chopped the ball, bunted, dragged, and all that stuff. It sure frustrated him when I used his methods."

By 1919, the fame of Rube Foster and his Chicago American Giants spanned all of America, as well as Canada and Cuba. Even the lowest paid players on the team were earning more than most middle-class Americans. Despite their bounty, however, Foster's athletes were always looking for a bigger paycheck. In one of a series of columns called "The Pitfalls of Baseball," which he wrote for the *Chicago Defender,* Foster complained about players jumping from team to team and about piracy among the owners. "Ball players," he wrote, "have no respect for their word, contracts or moral obligations, yet they are not nearly as much to blame as the different owners of clubs."

After WWI, white teams such as the Logan Squares and the Duffy Florals suffered a decline in popularity and subsequent loss of drawing power. Therefore, in addition to his roster problems, Foster suffered financial losses because the American Giants depended heavily on income derived from playing these teams.

Seeking a remedy to the problems of black baseball, and perhaps to some of his own personal problems, Foster proposed in one of his columns for the *Defender* the formation of Negro leagues patterned after the major leagues. One league, in the Midwest, would include Chicago, Cincinnati, Detroit, St. Louis, Kansas City, and Indianapolis. The other, in the East, would be made of Cleveland, Baltimore, Philadelphia, Pittsburgh, New York, and Washington. While Foster met staunch resistance in the East, the midwestern owners met in Kansas City on February 13, 1920, to form a league.

Elwood Knox of the *Indianapolis Freeman,* David Wyatt of the *Indianapolis Ledger,* and attorney Elisha Scott worked through the night to write the constitution for the proposed Negro National League. (In 1954, Scott would argue and win the historic *Brown v. Board of Education* case before the United States Supreme Court, ending legal segregation in America's public schools.)

The next day, Foster, representing the American Giants, the Dayton Marcos, and the Cuban Stars, signed the new constitution. He was joined by the owners of the Indianapolis ABCs, the Chicago Giants, the Detroit Stars, the St. Louis Giants, and the Kansas City Monarchs. Although Foster wanted an entirely black league, he did allow the entrance of the Monarchs, even though they were owned by a white man, J. L. Wilkinson. Ironically, Wilkinson would later emerge as one of the true giants of black baseball.

The NNL's constitution banned the league's owners from raiding each other's teams, and it prohibited players from jumping by implementing a reserve clause that bound them to their clubs. It even established a system of fines for less than exemplary conduct either on or off the field.

While most of the Eastern teams shunned Foster's NNL, the Philadelphia Hilldales and the Atlantic City Bacharachs became associate members of the league. Rube considered these Eastern connections very important because he wanted to conclude each season with a Black World Series. He hoped this would lead to a World Championship Series between the winners of the black major league and the white major leagues. Foster viewed both the Black World Series and the World Championship Series as preliminary steps along the path to integration.

The American Giants won the NNL's first pennant in 1920 and traveled east to play the Bacharachs in the series. Each team won two games, but for some unexplained reason no deciding contest was played.

While winning the pennant again in 1921, the American Giants made believers of everyone with an incredible comeback against the Indianapolis ABCs. After seven innings, the ABCs led 18–0. Instead of having his men hit, however, Foster gave the bunt sign 11 times in a row. The strategy panicked the ABCs' infield and American Giant runners swarmed all over the bases. Cristobal Torriente and Jim Brown each hit two grand slams, and the Chicagoans tied the score at 18–18 before the game was called because of darkness.

Following the season, the American Giants went East again, this time to meet the Hilldale club in a series played in Philadelphia's Shibe Park. The Fostermen went to work in the very first inning when Bobby Williams and Bingo DeMoss pulled a double steal. Williams then scored on Torriente's squeeze bunt. Torriente drilled a long homer in the fourth, but the speedsters returned in the sixth when Jimmy Lyons singled and then swiped second, third, and home. Williams did the same in the eighth, as the American Giants won 5–4, with ten steals. Unintimidated, Hilldale won the next three games. Foster and his men went on to battle the Bacharachs to a dead heat in a nine game series, one contest ending in a tie.

In 1922, the American Giants won another pennant and this time playing at home in Chicago, defeated the Bacharachs. Even as Foster prospered, however, and his league continued to stabilize, other men tried to emulate his success. On December 16, the Eastern Colored League was established. It was composed of Hilldale, the Bacharachs, the Brooklyn Royal Giants, the Lincoln Giants, the Baltimore Black Sox, and Alex Pompez's Cuban Stars of New York.

The Eastern League owners raided the NNL's rosters and inflicted serious damage. Foster himself lost his ace left-hander, Dave Brown, to the New York Lincoln Giants. Brown had joined the American Giants in 1918, when Foster had posted a $20,000 bond to secure his release from prison, where he was serving time for robbery. Brown did well under Foster's custody, but once in New York, he murdered a man in a cocaine dispute. Escaping to California, he was murdered himself.

Although the Kansas City Monarchs won the 1923 NNL pennant, no World Series was played because of hostile feelings between East and West. The Monarchs won again in 1924, and their owner, J. L. Wilkinson, challenged the eastern champion Hilldales to a World Series. Despite his dislike of Ed Bolden, owner of the Hilldale club, and his even more intense dislike of Nat Strong, the East's powerful booking agent, Foster attended the series and was cordial.

The Monarch-Hilldale matchup is considered the first true Black World Series. It went 10 games, with the Monarchs winning 5 games to 4, with one 13-inning tie. Aging Jose Mendez, the great Cuban right-hander, won the finale 5–0, as Foster sat on the bench with Wilkinson's permission and called every pitch. Young third baseman Judy Johnson hit .364 to lead both teams, with six doubles, a triple, and a home run among his 16 hits.

Foster continued to administer every aspect of operations for the NNL and for his own club. He kept the league alive by the sheer power and vitality of his personality as well as through various administrative and financial moves. Trying to maintain the league's parity, he sometimes dispatched his own players to other clubs. He also worked to sustain each team's financial integrity, even if it meant reaching into his own pocket.

Rube also continued his efforts to attain integration. Early in 1926, he met with President Ban Johnson of the American League and his old friend John McGraw to discuss the possibility of the American Giants playing any major league team which had a free day in Chicago.

Unfortunately, the long hours and stress exacted their toll and Foster began to lose his sanity. He hallucinated about pitching in a World Series game, ran after imaginary fly balls outside his apartment on Michigan Avenue, and hit a pedestrian while driving his flashy Apperson Jackrabbit. Eventually, he lost his ability

The Great Shortstop Willie Wells in 1929.

to function and spent the four remaining years of his life in the insane asylum at Kankakee, Illinois, a community south of Chicago. Until he died, on December 9, 1930, he raved about winning another pennant.

In 1926, David Malarcher did lead the American Giants to the NNL pennant and a subsequent victory over the Bacharachs in the World Series. Sadly, Foster didn't comprehend.

During the final services for Foster, the funeral parlor at 47th and Lawrence overflowed. Many of the 3000 mourners had to stand outside in chill rain and snow. Floral pieces abounded, some of them spectacular. The NNL's owners presented a 200-pound baseball composed of white chrysanthemums and red roses for seams. The American Giants Booster association offered a huge green wreath depicting a baseball diamond and displaying Foster's initials under a ball and crossed bats.

Among those standing outside were Cool Papa Bell and the great shortstop Willie Wells. They had traveled by bus from St. Louis to pay their final respects to a friend. Cool Papa remembers, "I guess we didn't mind standing out in the cold. They played Rock of Ages and I cried. So did Willie, but we weren't alone. There was a long procession and we walked all the way to Lincoln Cemetery."

While the Great Depression spelled doom for Rube Foster's Negro National League, his vision of baseball integration never died. We can see the fruition of his dream in the contemporary major leagues.

Several owners worked to keep Foster's vision alive after his death, including Cum Posey of the Homestead Grays and J. L. Wilkinson of the Kansas City Monarchs. In Pittsburgh, another man sat in the wings ready to resurrect the NNL. His name was Gus Greenlee. Most people called him "Big Red."

3

Big Red's Dream

Gus Greenlee had little formal education, but he
was wise in the ways of the street. He was a
gambler, a promoter, and a really fine guy.
Everybody called him "Big Red."

Ted Page, 1983
Pittsburgh, Pennsylvania

Cumberland Willis Posey was the resourceful owner/manager of the Homestead Grays, a black team situated in the southeastern Pittsburgh suburb of Homestead. Posey remained aloof from both Rube Foster's NNL and from the Eastern League. He valued his independence and seldom jeopardized his position with outside ventures. As the 1930s began, he had put together a powerhouse club featuring Joe Williams, Oscar Charleston, Josh Gibson, and Judy Johnson. Basking in the sunshine of his success, Posey failed to notice Gus Greenlee's thunder booming across his beloved Pittsburgh.

William A. "Gus" Greenlee came to Pittsburgh in 1920 from Marion, North Carolina, after serving in Europe during World War I. He decided to establish himself in the numbers game and financed his operation with the help of Harlem's leading black gangster Alex Pompez, owner of the Cuban Stars. Gus also fattened his bank account by hijacking liquor trucks in Pennsylvania and New York.

In 1925, having established himself as the numbers king of Pittsburgh's black community, Greenlee purchased the Crawford Grille on Wylie Avenue in the heart of the city's Hill District. The Grille, a sprawling two-story cabaret and restaurant, served the best food in the city, and it held sway as Pittsburgh's version of Harlem's Cotton Club. At night, the Grille swung to the sweet sounds of Count Basie, Duke Ellington, Cab Calloway, Lena Horne, the Mills Brothers, and other noted black musicians. It soon became the meeting place for Pittsburgh's most exciting personalities, black and white, a rich mix of gangsters, politicians, entertainers, and sports figures.

The Grille also served as headquarters for Greenlee's numbers runners. In the numbers game, or the policy wheel as it was often called, a gambler picked any three-digit number, and if it matched the predetermined number for the day, such as the last three digits of the race track handle, the organization paid off at odds of 500-to-1. By betting as little as a penny, a person could win $5. This represented big money for common people, especially as the Great Depression rolled across America.

Despite the gangster atmosphere, the black community attached no stigma to the numbers racket. Thus, Gus Greenlee enjoyed both respect and a flashy lifestyle that focused on the best food, the liveliest entertainment, the most expensive clothes, a new Lincoln convertible every year, and endless rounds of gambling.

Gus Greenlee, Founder of the Pittsburgh
Crawfords.

Greenlee surrounded himself with a streetwise organization, kingpinned by
the sophisticated Teddy Horne, Lena Horne's father. Teddy, who was well-
established in Pittsburgh's gambling community, supervised Greenlee's numbers
racket as well as his thriving liquor business.

From time to time, Jack Johnson also profited from some of the liquor action.
Johnson, however, wanted to move into the more lucrative drug business. He
even approached Cool Papa Bell, the epitome of respectability, to front a hotel
where drugs could be sold behind the scenes. Obviously, big Jack had to look
elsewhere.

While Pittsburgh's black population found no problem with Greenlee's gangster
activities, he was expected to provide significant financial support for the community. More than anything else, this meant sponsoring a baseball team. Therefore, in 1930, Big Red began bankrolling one of Pittsburgh's best black semi-pro

clubs, the Crawford Colored Giants. The Crawfords seemed a natural choice because they were sponsored by the Crawford Recreation Center located closed to Greenlee's headquarters at the Grille. He dreamed of turning the Crawfords into a black baseball dynasty, and in 1931, he began using his substantial bankroll to pursue his dream. Realizing the need for a ball park closer to the black community, he began construction of a new stadium complex at 2500 Bedford Avenue.

Completed during the late winter of 1932, Greenlee Field cost the numbers king a cool 100 grand. Beautiful, with a seating capacity of 7,500, the park sported a playing surface as lush and spacious as any major league field. Most significant of all, the complex included superb locker room facilities for both home and visiting clubs. No longer did black players have to dress and shower in the dingy atmosphere of the Pittsburgh YMCA because the white managers of Ammon Field or Forbes Field refused to let them use their sacred establishments.

As his first baseball employee, Greenlee hired John Clark as team secretary and publicist. With this brilliant move, Greenlee converted a stinging adversary into a valuable member of his organization. Clark had authored several blistering articles for the *Pittsburgh American* denouncing the numbers racket. Now, Greenlee owned Clark's powerful pen.

Even as Big Red began to mold his baseball empire, he also began to move into the boxing game, building up a stable of ten fighters. One of his men, John Henry Lewis, won the light-heavy title in 1935 by outpointing Bob Olin in St. Louis. In 1939, having defeated all the serious challengers in his division, John Henry fought his close friend Joe Louis for the heavyweight crown. Few besides Louis knew that John Henry was going blind. The Brown Bomber gave him the fight for one last big payday and mercifully knocked him out in the first round.

Even as Gus assembled his boxing stable, he began to fill his baseball stable as well. Late in 1931, he obtained the first of his franchise players. For a mere $250, he purchased the contract of Leroy "Satchel" Paige from the Cleveland Cubs. By the summer of 1931, Paige neared dominance among black pitchers with his exquisite control and with the enormous velocity of his humming "bee" ball overpowering most opposition.

Early in 1932, Greenlee picked up the spitballing left-hander Sam Streeter. He also made a splendid acquisition with the signing of outfielder Jimmie Crutchfield, a small speedy package of dynamite from Moberly, Missouri.

Gus then began unlimbering his bank account in full pursuit of the cream of Posey's Homestead Grays, who were suffering hard financial times because of the Depression. Lured by more money and by a chance to play for an organization

Manager Oscar Charleston, Rap Dixon, Josh
Gibson, Judy Johnson, and Jud Wilson. This
group comprised the heart of the Crawfords'
lineup during their first season in 1932.

that promised to be the classiest in all of black baseball, the brilliant veteran Oscar
Charleston joined the Crawfords to manage and play first base. Third baseman
Judy Johnson moved over with Charleston, as did catcher Josh Gibson, the mur-
derous young slugger who had slammed 75 homers for the Grays in 1931.

Greenlee also acquired speedy outfielder Ted Page from the Grays, along with
infielder Jud Wilson, second baseman John Henry Russell, and catcher Bill Perkins, who inscribed on his chest protector, "Thou Shalt Not Steal." The versatile
Ted "Double Duty" Radcliffe also switched clubs. He had earned his unusual
nickname by pitching the first game of a doubleheader and catching the second.

On February 18, the Crawfords left for spring training in Hot Springs, Arkansas. They traveled in a new Mack bus, which was a beautiful machine and quite
comfortable for its time. Despite his huge frame, at 6'2'' and 225 pounds, Greenlee
managed to squeeze into the driver's seat and do some of the chauffeuring himself.

Rather than playing in an organized league, Greenlee decided the Crawfords could make more money by barnstorming. They played their first game in Monroe, Louisiana, on March 25, and by July 21, they had played 94 games all over the South, running up 117,000 miles on the Mack. Clark, writing for the *Pittsburgh Courier,* provided the home fans with lively accounts of the team's marvelous string of victories. He also commented on the social conditions of blacks in the South.

Everywhere they went, the Crawfords opened eyes with their talent and with their class. They rolled into towns with a new bus, a team secretary, tailored uniforms, and excellent equipment. Most Southerners had never seen a team so close to major league status.

In Houston, Texas, a Creole woman named Mother Mitchell provided dinner for the entire club. With an income of $25,000 a month in oil royalties, she could afford to entertain in spectacular fashion. Jimmie Crutchfield recalls the evening. "You talk about a feast. It was the fanciest affair of my life."

Cool Papa also remembers the evening. "This lady lived in a fine old southern house. It had a huge dining room, big enough to seat the whole team. It had fine furniture, thick rugs, and several crystal chandeliers on the ceiling.

"What a meal we had. There was roast beef and fried chicken. Mashed potatoes and sweet potatoes. Home-baked bread. Several kinds of salad. For dessert, we had our choice of several kinds of pies and fruit of all kinds.

"What a night we had. I'll never forget it. We didn't eat too well on the road you know. So many places wouldn't even serve us. When we got back to Pittsburgh, Judy Johnson and I wrote her a letter thanking her for her hospitality."

Meanwhile, back in Pittsburgh, Cum Posey waited for revenge. The intense rivalry between the Crawfords and the Grays sparked great interest among the fans, and the *Courier* fanned the fires for weeks in advance of a confrontation between the two powerhouses. The teams themselves encouraged the rivalry because it meant more money in the till. To avoid Pennsylvania's Sunday blue laws, Gus once spent $6,000 on portable lights for Greenlee Field and the two teams began a game at 12:01 A.M. The Grays won before dawn.

Despite Greenlee's plundering of talent, the Grays defeated the Crawfords ten times in nineteen tries during the 1932 season. Still, the fans no longer considered the Grays Pittsburgh's most exciting black baseball team. Their hearts belonged to the dazzling Crawfords.

In October, led by Ted Page's hot bat and Satchel Paige's brilliant pitching, the Crawfords concluded a successful season by defeating Casey Stengel's All-Stars five games out of seven. Despite Stengel's strong pitching staff and the presence of Hack Wilson, who had hit 56 homers for the Chicago Cubs in 1930, the Crawfords handled the big leaguers with relative ease.

During the off-season, Greenlee reconsidered his feelings about barnstorming. Hoping to improve his finances and further solidify his legitimacy in the eyes of the common people, he decided to preside over the restoration of the Negro National League which had folded after the 1931 season because of Rube Foster's death and because of the Depression.

In January, Gus met with other team owners and formed the second NNL. It opened with the Crawfords, the Chicago American Giants, the Columbus Blue Birds, the Detroit Stars, and the Indianapolis ABCs. Before the middle of the season, the ABCs folded. They were replaced by the Baltimore Black Sox and the Nashville Elite Giants.

The NNL operated on a split-season schedule, and the Chicago American Giants won the first-half pennant by one game over the Crawfords. When the second-half schedule was not completed, the American Giants claimed the season's championship. As league chairman, however, Greenlee exercised his power and declared his own Crawfords the champions.

Greenlee understood power, of course, and he knew the NNL needed a substantial infusion of money. Big Red knew just where to go. Over the years under his leadership, the league became a stronghold of the wealthiest and most powerful black gangsters in America. Eager to launder racket money, Ed "Soldier Boy" Semler financed the New York Black Yankees; Ed Bolden the Philadelphia Stars; Tom Wilson, the Baltimore Elite Giants; Abe and Effa Manley, the Newark Eagles; and Alex Pompez, the New York Cubans.

Cum Posey refused to join Greenlee's NNL until 1935 when he also found himself in need of gangster money. His support came from Rufus "Sonnyman" Jackson who ran the notorious night roll in Homestead and also masterminded most of the early jukebox action up and down the Allegheny and Monongahela Rivers.

Despite the shortcomings of the new league, as well as the questionable activities of the man himself, Greenlee emerged as a positive force for black baseball. In 1933, he founded the East-West All-Star classic, and while he demanded 10 percent of the profit, the remaining proceeds provided financial grace for some teams that might have otherwise succumbed to depression economics. Furthermore, the game exposed black talent to those white men who would later open the doors to integration.

Greenlee also realized that in order to attain real success, the NNL must have a strong organization to support necessary reforms. Players showed little respect for contracts or for umpires. The lack of respect for umpires extended beyond arguments to cursing, pushing, and even shoving. Sam Streeter even remembered umpires being threatened by fans with guns and knives.

Respect for umpires definitely increased over the years, but the NNL made little progress in upgrading the integrity of contracts. Greenlee's overall efforts did prove successful, however, as the NNL survived with some degree of prosperity until 1948.

Big Red achieved even more success on the field. As the 1933 season neared, he knew the Crawfords needed a great center fielder to become the best team in black baseball. The Depression doomed the remarkable St. Louis Stars, and Cum Posey picked up the best of their players for the Detroit Wolves, a team he maintained in addition to the Grays. The Wolves' roster included four former Stars, power hitter Mule Suttles, brilliant shortstop Willie Wells, left-handed pitcher Leroy Matlock, and Cool Papa Bell, the best outfielder in black baseball. Greenlee signed both Bell and Matlock.

It seems strange, however, that Gus bypassed Suttles and Wells. Suttles ranked in the same class as Gibson as a power hitter, and next to John Henry Lloyd, Wells was the best shortstop in black baseball history. The addition of Suttles and Wells would have made the Crawfords the best baseball team ever, black or white. Even more strange is the fact that Posey offered no resistance to Greenlee's signing of Bell and Matlock or to Suttles and Wells moving on to the Chicago American Giants.

As the 1933 season began, the Crawfords stood poised on the threshold of a golden age. The heart of their lineup, with Paige on the mound, Gibson behind the plate, Charleston at first, Johnson at third, and Bell in the outfield, flanked by Jimmie Crutchfield and Ted Page, was ready to make Big Red's dream come true.

4

Master Satch

Satchel Paige was the best and fastest pitcher I ever
faced.

Joe DiMaggio, 1979
Springfield, Illinois

Satchel Paige's reputation loomed so large that when the young Joe DiMaggio managed an infield hit against him in 1935, he proudly proclaimed that he was ready for the major leagues. While Satchel encouraged people to speculate about his age, his talent remained above dispute. Besides DiMaggio, many others, including Jimmie Foxx, Charlie Gehringer, Dizzy Dean, and Bill Veeck, believed Paige was the best ever. In 1934, Satchel matched up with Dean in what Veeck called the greatest game he ever saw. Dean, a 30-game winner with the World Champion St. Louis Cardinals, held the Pittsburgh Crawfords to one run and fanned 15. Paige shutout the Dean Stars while whiffing 17.

During the 1930s and 1940s, the name of Satchel Paige became synonymous with black baseball and it remains so to this day. Like Babe Ruth, Paige's exploits both on and off the field created continuous excitement. He stood larger than life, and people came to expect the extraordinary from him.

Paige pitched an estimated 2,500 games during his career, winning approximately 2,000 of them. The 2,000 wins included some 250 shutouts and 50 no-hitters. In 1935, he pitched 29 days in a row against powerful teams and lost only once. During the winter seasons of 1932–1936 while pitching against the best of the black players (as well as major leaguers), he lost only four games.

Fiercely independent, eccentric, and unpredictable, Paige inspired much jealousy among his contemporaries. Still, most found it impossible to dislike him. According to Jimmie Crutchfield, "Satchel had a wonderful personality. When he came into the ballpark it was like the sun coming out."

"People just didn't understand him," says Cool Papa Bell. "Nobody could tell him what to do. Some people didn't like that independence and some were very jealous of his baseball ability too."

The Master emerged from inauspicious beginnings. Born in Mobile, Alabama, on July 7, 1906, he grew up in a "shotgun" house, where the four rooms were a straight shot from the front to the back. He shared the house with ten brothers and sisters. His father, John Page, was a gardener, while his mother, Lula, was a domestic. According to Satchel, "My parents changed the family name to Paige so it would sound more high tone."

While working as a seven-year-old porter of suitcases and satchels at the Mobile train depot, Paige earned his lifelong nickname. At age 8, he began throwing in earnest, becoming quite proficient at hitting almost any target with a rock. Two years later, he starred as a pitcher for the W. H. Council Elementary School in Mobile.

Satchel Paige in 1935.

Unfortunately, Satchel spent most of his time getting into trouble by playing hookey or fighting. In July 1918, he stole some small toys from a store and was committed to the Industrial School for Negro Children at Mount Meigs, Alabama. Satchel spent five years at the reformatory and he claimed, "My time there made me a man. I played ball, sang in the choir, and got a pretty fair education."

Following his release in 1923, Paige began pitching for the local semi-pro team, the Mobile Tigers, for $1 a game. In 1926, after three years with the Tigers, during which time he went virtually undefeated, Satchel signed his first professional contract with the Chattanooga Black Lookouts of the Negro Southern League. He earned a mere $50 a month and began to develop a bitterness about his lack of opportunity to pitch in the major leagues. "I kept thinkin' how I'd like to pitch against Babe Ruth," he said. "Eventually, I got my chance."

Paige pitched for the Birmingham Black Barons in 1928, and for the Nashville Elite Giants in 1929, 1930, and 1931. Following the 1930 season, he pitched in Nashville against his first major leaguers, a hard-hitting group of barnstormers led by Babe Herman and Hack Wilson. He shut them out with 22 strikeouts.

Cool Papa Bell first saw The Master in Nashville. "Oooee," he says, "Satch was really somethin'. He was tall you know, between 6'3" and 6'4", but he only weighed about 180, so it seemed like he was all arms and legs. He could put that big fastball right at your knees all day long. It seemed to come right out of his big foot. Great speed. Great control.

"I actually hit him pretty well. I used a half swing, because you just couldn't get around on him. Satch loved to pitch against those guys with the big swings. He'd just throw it right by 'em."

"I do remember one time when none of us could hit him. I was leading off and before the first pitch he said, 'I'm not gonna throw any fast ones today. All you're gonna get is slow stuff. And that's just what we got. Know what? He shut us out. We kept lookin' for the fastball in key spots, but we never got it. Satch laughed at us all day long."

The Elite Giants, who sometimes played as the Cleveland Cubs, disbanded after the 1931 season because of financial problems, and Gus Greenlee signed Paige for the Crawfords. This began a stormy, but mutually profitable relationship.

On April 29, 1932, Satchel pitched in Greenlee Field's debut against the New York Black Yankees and their pitching ace, Mountain Jesse Hubbard. Unfortunately for the Crawfords, Hubbard and his teammates prevailed 1–0 when center fielder Clint Thomas made a spectacular game-saving grab of Josh Gibson's towering drive. Later in the season, Paige avenged his defeat with a brilliant no-hitter at the expense of the Black Yankees.

Greenlee, a natural promoter, began advertising Paige as the "World's Greatest Pitcher," and Gibson as the "World's Greatest Hitter." His advertising promised that Satchel would strike out the first nine men and Josh would hit a home run. Many times, the billing proved correct. Once, when the Crawfords played an exhibition game in Jonesboro, Arkansas, the two men carried the advertising to an extreme. Satchel struck out the first 13 men and Josh hit three homers.

Paige, with a natural flair for showmanship, needed little help with promotion. His baseball talent, combined with colorful speech and a flamboyant life-style, soon made him the darling of Pittsburgh's black sportswriters. He often delighted his admirers by placing a gum wrapper on home plate and then firing his fastball across it time after time.

The Master also expanded his pitching repertoire. In addition to his natural three-quarter motion, he began throwing overhand, sidearm, and submarine. He also supplemented his fastball, which he now called the "Long Tom," with a blooper as well as a baffling hesitation pitch in which he stopped midway through his motion before serving up the pitch.

At the Crawford Grille, Paige almost always reigned as the life of the party. He could sing, dance, play a variety of instruments, and shoot pool with the best. The musicians loved him, the pool sharks respected him, and the ladies followed him everywhere. Janet Howard, a resourceful waitress at the Grille, followed him to the end of the trail. "From the first time she set a plate of asparagus down in front of me," Satchel recalled, "I knew my bachelor days were about over."

Satchel married Janet, a diminutive beauty whom everyone affectionately called "Toadalo," on October 26, 1934. Greenlee hosted both the ceremony and reception at the Grille, with Bill "Bojangles" Robinson serving as the best man and providing the entertainment. The marriage lasted until 1943.

Toadalo, along with everyone else, had trouble keeping track of Satchel. One day, Gus Greenlee visited the boxing gym where John Henry Lewis trained. Much to his chagrin, he saw his two most expensive employees in the ring together. Paige, clad in brightly colored boxing shorts, circled Lewis looking for a chance to land a good punch. Sadly, he succeeded in clipping Lewis on the chin, whereupon John Henry knocked him cold with a left hook to the jaw. After being revived, Paige beamed. "I sure stung him," he said. "Now, I want a shot at Joe Louis."

Paige neither feared the heavyweight champion, nor the U.S. Marine Corps. One time, during an exhibition game with the Crawfords beating the Leathernecks 12–0, Josh Gibson came to the mound.

"This is really unpatriotic," said Gibson.

"I agree," replied Paige. "The Marines have to score at least one run."

Satchel then served up a fat bug to a surprised Marine who hit a slow roller in front of the plate. Gibson scooped up the ball and fired it way down the right field line. As the runner circled the bases, the right fielder retrieved the errant throw and fired it home just before he reached home plate. The ball hit Gibson's chest protector and bounced away. The Crawfords won by a score of 12–1.

After the game, Gibson told the Marine captain, "I had a feeling you were going to be a hero."

Some of Paige's Crawford teammates resented his arrogance, however. One time during the 1932 season, when he filled the bases with nobody out, Judy Johnson came over and said, "Some of the boys were hoping you'd get yourself in this spot. They think you've got a big mouth."

Satchel said nothing, but proceeded to strikeout the side on the next nine pitches.

Returning to the bench, and eager to get in the last word, Satchel said, "The next time that happens, I'll just ask you boys to take a seat on the bench while I take care of the situation."

While Paige's unpredictability irritated some, it remained a source of amusement to others. Cool Papa Bell remembers a strange incident. "At the end of the 1937 winter season in California, Satchel offered to give me his car. He bought it when he first got to the Coast that year. It was a bright green Packard convertible that had belonged to some movie star. Bette Davis I think. Anyway, it cost a whole lot of money. My wife Clara and I were out in front of the hotel waiting for a taxi to take us to the bus depot. Satchel came up and said, 'Hey, Cool, how would you and Clara like to have my car? You can drive it back to St. Louis and keep it.' Well, neither of us drove. We always used public transportation. So, I said no thanks. He just dropped the keys in the front seat and walked away. 'I'm sure somebody will appreciate it,' he said. I still laugh about that time."

Paige finished with a 21–7 record for the Crawfords in 1932, and in 1933, he rolled up an astonishing 31–4. Greenlee also loaned him out as a drawing card to other teams, with the two of them dividing the profits.

Paige continued his brilliant pitching during the 1934 season, including an overpowering no-hitter against the Homestead Grays on July 4. Late in the year, however, he became involved in a salary dispute with Greenlee and jumped his Crawfords' contract in favor of employment with the white Bismarck, North Dakota, club. Under the dynamic leadership of Mayor Neil Churchill, the city of Bismarck was in the process of establishing its team as a baseball powerhouse, especially because of a willingness to accept integrated baseball. Unfortunately, many in the Bismarck community failed to share the liberal attitude of their baseball patrons. Satchel and Toadalo thus found themselves living in a railroad boxcar.

Additionally, many of Paige's new teammates seemed inclined to doubt his ability. He proceeded to establish himself right away. Asking them to watch, he placed a small matchbox on an upright stick behind home plate. He then knocked the matchbox off the stick with 15 of 20 pitches from the mound. Having proven his control, Satchel then unleashed his great speed, overpowering a catcher time after time with his Long Tom.

Paige's first pitching test came against Bismarck's principal rival, the neighboring Jamestown Red Sox. The Master barely worked up a sweat in shutting them out with 15 strikeouts. He used only his Little Tom, the medium fastball, saving Long Tom for future games.

Paige did lose one game to Jamestown, however. He later recalled the strange circumstances surrounding the defeat.

"All through the year," he said, "I had sometimes called my outfield in and finished an inning with just my infielders. The fans loved it. My signal for the boys to come in was when I turned my back to the plate and wiped my hand across my forehead.

"Well, on that night, Jamestown was hittin' everything I threw up there. But we were hittin' too, so we were ahead something like 15 to 14 in the bottom of the ninth. With two outs, their number three hitter singled and up came their cleanup man. I was worried and without thinkin', I turned my back to the batter and wiped the sweat off my head. I turned back to the plate and pitched without even lookin' at the outfield. But the boys out there thought I wanted them to come in. I threw the big guy a little curve on the outside edge up high so he would pop the ball to the right side. He did. I turned to watch the final out with a big grin on my face. But there was no outfield; they were just about all the way off the field. The ball went into right field and rolled so far that both men scored and they won the game. I was a might embarrassed. The fans weren't too happy about that one."

When a furious Gus Greenlee banned him from the Crawfords in 1935, Paige returned to Bismarck for the summer. The team won 97 while losing only 5, with Satchel posting a 43–2 record. In one stretch, he pitched 29 days in a row and lost only once.

In the fall, a group of major leaguers, powered by Earl Averill, Heinie Manush, and Jimmie Foxx, all future Hall-of-Famers, appeared in North Dakota ready to have some fun with the locals. When they found out Paige was there, they knew there would be little fun. Bismarck beat the big leaguers 16–2 at home, 7–4 at Grand Forks, and 10–0 at Valley City. At Bismarck, Paige fanned the muscular Foxx three times. Instead of making excuses, Foxx only expressed his relief that he didn't have to face Satchel during the regular season.

North Dakota then, as now, was home to many Sioux Indians. The Sioux, fascinated by Paige, called him the Long Rifle. He recalled an incident among them which he says helped him have such a long career.

"One day," he said, "Dorothy Running Deer invited me to her home. When I saw that her father raised rattlesnakes in a deep pit behind his house, I was ready to say goodbye. Before I left, I asked the old man if he had ever been bitten by one of the rattlers. He told me that he had been bitten many times, but that he had an ointment that protected him. He gave me a big jug of the stuff and I asked him if it would be good for rubbin' on my arm. He told me no.

"A few days later, I worked up my courage and tried some of it. My mistake was that I didn't dilute it. Man, I thought my arm was gonna fly outta the room. I had to go back a couple of times for more, but I used the stuff for many years. I think it helped me pitch as long as I did."

Bismarck's National Semi-Pro Champions,
1935. Satchel Paige standing, back row center.

Following the 1935 season, and their destruction of the major leaguers, Bismarck left North Dakota to play in the national semipro tournament in Wichita, Kansas. On route through the Sunflower state, the team was challenged by the local club in McPherson. Bismarck won 2–0, but as the last inning began, the fans made the mistake of riding Satchel real hard. He responded by fanning the first batter and then calling in the outfield while he struck out the second. He finished the show by calling in the infield and striking out the last hitter. He used just nine pitches to dispatch the three men. Bismarck went on to win the Wichita tournament in seven games.

Gus Greenlee, enraged by the jump to Bismarck, maintained that Paige could never return to the Crawfords. Satchel's charm helped change his mind, as did the Crawfords' financial problems. After all, The Master was Greenlee's biggest drawing card.

Paige pitched for the Crawfords in 1936, but the next spring, as the Crawfords' financial situation grew dark, he once more became a traveling man. Following the Sun south, he pitched during the summer of 1937 for dictator Rafael Trujillo's team in the Dominican Republic.

Paige pitched the 1938 season in the Mexican League and there, for the first time in his career, he developed a sore arm. Strangely, Satchel blamed his arm problems on his sensitive stomach, which reacted poorly to the spicy Mexican food. He believed the problems originated in his digestive tract and spread to his pitching arm. Even the snake oil didn't help, and an American physician advised him that he would never pitch again.

During the winter, the Kansas City Monarchs offered Satchel a place on their second team, which was a barnstorming club. Billing themselves as Satchel Paige's All-Stars, the team played all over Canada and the American Northwest. The suffering Paige pitched an inning or two at the beginning of every game, trying to get batters out with a variety of slow stuff.

Then one day for no apparent reason the big fastball returned. Satchel immediately became the pitching mainstay of the Monarch's big team, leading them to the Negro American League pennant each year from 1939 to 1942.

In 1942, the Monarchs met the Homestead Grays, champions of the Negro National League, in the first Black World Series since 1927. The Monarchs won the series in five games, with Satchel picking up three of the four victories.

Also during the 1942 season, Paige had his historic showdown with Josh Gibson. Paige and Gibson had always been friendly rivals, and on July 21 at Forbes Field in Pittsburgh, black baseball's best pitcher went "mano a mano" with black baseball's greatest hitter.

Paige and the Monarchs led the Grays 4–0 after six innings. After retiring the first two hitters in the seventh, Satchel gave up a triple to Jerry Benjamin.

Paige called first baseman Buck O'Neil to the mound. "Hey Nancy," yelled Paige, using his pet nickname for O'Neil, "I'm gonna walk Howard Easterling and Buck Leonard. I wanna pitch to Josh with the bases drunk."

"C'mon Satch," said O'Neil, "you've got to be crazy."

As usual, Satchel listened to nobody but himself. He proceeded to walk Easterling and Leonard on eight pitches.

When Gibson stepped to the plate, Satchel yelled down to him, "Hey Josh, remember years ago when I said, 'You're the greatest hitter in Negro baseball and I'm the greatest pitcher. Someday, we're gonna see who's best.' Well, this is the time. Let's see who wins this one."

"Josh, I'm gonna tell you exactly what I'm going to throw," continued Paige. "I'm not gonna trick you. I'm gonna start by giving you a fastball."

The Long Tom boomed in knee high. Josh took it for strike one.

"Now, I'm gonna throw you another fastball, but it's gonna be faster than the first."

Another Long Tom zipped in at the knees. Once more, Josh just looked. Strike two.

"Now, my man Josh, that's two strikes. I'm still not gonna trick you. I'm not gonna throw any smoke around your yoke. I'm gonna throw a pea at your knee, only it's gonna be even faster than the first two."

The crowd grew silent. Gibson steeled himself for the big pitch. Satchel wound, double pumped, put his big foot in Josh's face, and fired another fastball knee high on the outside corner. Josh froze. He was called out on strikes without ever having swung the bat.

A legend now, Paige worked for the Monarchs for the next five seasons. Instead of pitching for the big team, however, the Kansas City owners most often hired him out to other teams as a gate attraction.

In 1948, Jackie Robinson, who the year before had become the first black player in the major leagues, reached for superstardom with the Brooklyn Dodgers. The stylish Larry Doby, who joined the Cleveland Indians late in 1947 as the American League's first black, now sparked his club both offensively at the plate and defensively from his position in the middle garden. The Master, forgotten by many, still pitched behind the white curtain.

As the Indians made a run for the pennant, team president Bill Veeck searched for some pitching insurance. Working with promoter Abe Saperstein, he found his insurance in Satchel Paige, but manager Lou Boudreau needed some convincing. During the last week in June, Paige journeyed to the big stadium on Lake Erie to show Mr. Lou his stuff. He threw fifty pitches. Forty-six of them were strikes. Lou believed.

Others remained doubters, however, including the venerable J. G. Taylor Spink, publisher of baseball's bible, the *Sporting News*. He wrote:

> Many well-wishers of baseball emphatically fail to see eye to eye with the signing of Satchel Paige, superannuated Negro pitcher. . . . To bring in a pitching rookie of Paige's age . . . is to demean the standards of baseball in the big circuits.

On July 9, 1948, Paige made his first big league pitching appearance. The 20,000 fans in Cleveland gave him a ten minute standing ovation. The Master responded by blanking the St. Louis Browns in two innings of relief.

In another of his initial relief appearances, Paige showed that he had lost none of his confidence. Called in to pitch against the legendary New York Yankees with nobody out, Satchel spied Phil Rizzuto on third waiting to score at the first opportunity. "Just relax, little man," he said to the Scooter, "you ain't goin' nowhere." Paige proceeded to retire the Yankees on ten pitches, stranding Rizzuto at third.

Satchel Paige

On August 13th, Satchel started his first game. The Chicago White Sox provided the opposition and 51,013 fans, the most ever to see a night game at Comiskey Park, filled the stadium. Outside, thousands surrounded the park and threatened to tear the gates down. Breaking through the police lines, thousands went around, over, and under the gates. They jammed together underneath the stands. Among those in attendance was the famous Detroit Brown Bomber, heavyweight champion Joe Louis.

"When I came down to the dugout from warming up," Satchel remembered, "Boudreau pointed over to the first row. I looked over and there was Joe Louis. I was truly honored to have him there to see me pitch. Old Satch didn't bow to many men, but he bowed to Joe Louis. He was such a great man. Such a kind man. He meant so much to black people."

Bill Veeck sat in nervous anticipation of the game. The newspapers had been pounding him because of his signing of Paige, with many calling it a cheap publicity stunt. Veeck stood by The Master through the storm and now hoped his "rookie" could vindicate both of them.

Saving his Long Tom for key spots, and thus preserving his energy, Satchel handcuffed the White Sox with a baffling assortment of slow stuff. He shut them out 5–0, allowing only five hits and giving no free passes.

A week later on August 20, Satchel started against the White Sox again, this time in Cleveland before 78,382, the largest crowd ever to see a night game up to that time. He hurled his second straight shutout, allowing only three hits, while striking out five and walking only one.

Paige made an important contribution to the Indians' American League pennant, with a 6–1 record, and a 2.48 earned run average. Several writers voted for him for Rookie of the Year. "I declined the position," Paige said. "I wasn't sure which year those gentlemen were referring to."

Sadly, as the Indians defeated the Boston Braves in the World Series, Satchel became the forgotten man, pitching only ⅔ of an inning. He remained bitter about this episode for the rest of his life, and he often commented, "I never went back to Cleveland."

Paige did return to Cleveland for the 1949 season, however. After he compiled a 4–7 record for the year, the Indians released him. The Master returned to barnstorming.

During the 1950 pennant drive, both the Boston Braves and the New York Giants offered Paige a contract. He turned them down. "I couldn't afford the cut in pay," Satchel said. "I was makin' twice as much on the road."

Then in the middle of the 1951 campaign, Veeck, then president of the St. Louis Browns, returned Paige to the American League. After compiling a 3–4 record, Satchel considered retiring.

When spring came, however, an eager Paige showed up at the Browns' spring training camp in Burbank, California. He turned out to be a workhorse from the bullpen, pitching almost every other day. By July 4, he had appeared in 25 games, and American League All-Star manager Casey Stengel of the New York Yankees picked him as one of his pitchers for the July dream game.

At the All-Star game, one of the reporters asked Satchel why he pitched so well against the great hitters, while at the same time, weak hitters seemed to own him. "Joe DiMaggio hit almost nothing against you," said the reporter. "Ted Williams and Mickey Mantle have only a few hits off you. But guys we've hardly even heard of smack you around. How come?"

"Well," said Satchel, "it's just like the old days. When I was pitchin' against Ruth, Gehrig, Foxx, Hornsby, guys like that, I really bore down. I struck those guys out a lot. It's simple, I just save my best pitchin' for the best hitters."

Paige put together an awesome season in 1952. He worked 46 games, winning 12, losing 10, and saving 10. In 1953, he made the All-Star team again, and saved another 11 games for the Browns. When Veeck left St. Louis, and the team moved to Baltimore, Paige was released again.

Satchel rejoined the Monarchs and continued his barnstorming career until 1956, when Veeck, then with the Miami club of the International League, signed him again. Paige went 11–4 that first year with Miami and posted a 1.86 earned run average. He stayed with the club through 1958.

Satchel pitched a short time for Portland of the Pacific Coast League in 1961, and in 1965, Charles Finley, owner of the Kansas City Athletics, hired him to pitch three innings against the Boston Red Sox. On September 25, 1965, Satchel pitched three scoreless innings against the Red Sox. At 59, he thus became the oldest man to appear in a major league game.

Among his many legacies, The Master left his formula for staying young:

1. Avoid fried meats which angry up the blood.
2. If your stomach disputes you, lie down and pacify it with cool thoughts.
3. Keep the juices flowing by jangling around gently as you move.
4. Go very light on the vices, such as carrying on in society. The social ramble ain't restful.
5. Avoid running at all times.
6. Don't look back. Something might be gaining on you.

5

*The Black
Bomber*

---

*I couldn't carry Josh's glove. Anything I could do,
he could do better.*

Roy Campanella, Hall of Fame Catcher
Brooklyn Dodgers

Joe Louis ruled boxing as the Brown Bomber, while Josh Gibson stood as baseball's Black Bomber. He may well have been the greatest power hitter in the game's history.

Once a young fan asked Josh if he could have one of his broken bats. "Son," replied the gentle Gibson, "I don't break bats, I wear them out. But I think I can find you one." Legend also has it that while playing for the Crawfords during the 1930s, Josh hit a ball so high and far that nobody saw it come down. The bewildered umpire ruled the ball a home run. The next day, when the Crawfords played in Philadelphia, a ball fell from the sky into the hands of the opposing center fielder. The same umpire pointed to Gibson and shouted, "You're out."

These stories seem to fall in the mythical realm of Babe Ruth squeezing sawdust from the end of his bat, or Bronko Nagurski running his own interference. Still, if anyone ever wore out bats or launched baseballs into space, Gibson was the man.

For instance, instead of Babe Ruth, or Lou Gehrig, or Mickey Mantle, Josh hit the longest home run in Yankee Stadium history. The *Sporting News* of June 3, 1967, verified Gibson's shot as landing just two feet from the top of the stadium wall that circled the bleachers in center field. The drive was estimated at 580 feet, and if it had gone two feet higher and left the park, the distance might well have been 700 feet or more.

Gibson also hit many tape-measure shots out of Washington's Griffith Stadium. The great Walter Johnson, after watching the big slugger play, told Senators' owner Clark Griffith, "Gibson is worth $250,000. He can do everything. He can hit the ball a mile, catch as if he was in a rocking chair, and throw like a rifle. Too bad he's a colored fellow."

As the Gibson legend spread, it became quite common for big leaguers to attend Negro League games just to see him hit. He inspired the same awe among both his teammates and his opponents around the black circuit. Cool Papa Bell still marvels about his hitting. "The first thing I remember about Josh," says Bell, "was his courage. Everybody threw at him and tried to scare him. It didn't ever work. He just concentrated more. I'm surprised they didn't stop throwin' at him, but they never gave up.

"I've seen all the power hitters in my time, Ruth, Foxx, Mantle, all of those guys. Most of them took long strides, waded into the ball, and took big swings. Many times, they could be fooled by pitchers who changed speeds because they were off-balance. Josh, on the other hand, had a short compact swing and took a

Josh Gibson in 1935.

very short stride. He was almost never off-balance, never fooled. He didn't just hit home runs you know. He also hit for a very high average. He hit over .400 many times for the season and hit over .400 against major league pitching. I'd say his lifetime average was something like .380 or .390.

"Josh reminded me of Lou Gehrig because he hit mostly line drives, instead of high fly balls like Ruth. Hank Aaron and Ernie Banks had swings like Josh, short and compact, with lots of wrist snap."

Joshua Gibson, was born in Buena Vista, Georgia, on December 21, 1911. His parents, Mark and Nancy, earned a meager living as sharecroppers. In 1921, Mark followed the great Negro migration to the North, hoping to find a better job to support his family, which included two other children besides Josh. Mark found work with the Carnegie-Illinois steel plant and, in 1924, he sent for his family.

Josh would later say that the move to the North side of Pittsburgh was "the best present my dad ever gave me."

Josh completed the fifth grade in Buena Vista and continued his education in Pittsburgh. He finished the ninth grade at the Allegheny Pre-Vocational School and then dropped out to become an apprentice at an air-brake factory. At the same time, Josh began to emerge as a great athlete in baseball, football, basketball, and swimming. As a swimmer, he won several medals in Pittsburgh's summer recreation program.

Gibson donned his first real baseball uniform at the age of 16, as a catcher for Gimbels Athletic Club, one of Pittsburgh's all-black amateur teams. Later, he moved on to the Crawford Colored Giants, a semipro club that charged no admission to its games, but picked up a few dollars by passing the hat. Josh earned about $2.00 a game.

By this time, Gibson neared his full size of 6'1" and 200 pounds. He had a classic athlete's body, with broad shoulders, great muscular arms, and a huge chest which tapered down to a slim waist. He exuded power. Cool Papa Bell remembers Gibson's strength. "Oscar Charleston," he says, "was very strong and everybody was afraid of him. Everybody except Josh. One time, Charleston and I got in an argument. I thought Charleston was gonna hit me. Before anything really happened, Josh came up and grabbed him in a headlock. Charleston couldn't do anything. Josh handled him like a baby. Charleston stayed clear of him from then on."

Judy Johnson remembered Gibson's beginning as a professional player with the Homestead Grays. "I started hearing about this young catcher all over town. He kept hitting 400- and 500-foot homers. People were saying they'd never seen a better hitter. Then, Josh started attending some of the Grays' games. I talked to him a little and found out that he was a wonderful sincere young man who wanted more than anything just to play baseball.

"One night in late July of 1929, when I was managing the Grays, we played a night game at Forbes Field against the Kansas City Monarchs. It wasn't an ordinary game because the Monarchs brought along a lighting system. They came in with 10 or 12 trucks carrying a whole bunch of lighting towers and a 250-horsepower engine for a generator. They set the towers up all around the field.

"One of the problems with the lights was that the towers weren't tall enough. The generator also sputtered a lot and then the lights would get dim. The players couldn't see the ball very well and it just wasn't the best playing situation.

"Because of the lights, we had to use different signals between the pitcher and the catcher. You couldn't see fingers, so we used glove up for the fastball and glove down for the curve. Well, Joe Williams was pitching that night and even though he was an old man, he could still throw some smoke. It wasn't long before he and

47

the catcher, Buck Ewing, got crossed up and Ewing split a finger. Vic Harris, my backup catcher was in left field, but when I asked him to come in and take over, he said, 'I'm not gonna catch Williams in candlelight. Find somebody else.'

"Well, it so happened that Josh was sitting in the stands that night. I asked Cum Posey, the Grays' owner, to ask him to finish the game behind the plate. Josh got real excited when Posey asked him. We got him into a uniform and he finished up for us. It wasn't long before he was our number one catcher.

"At first, he was a terrible receiver. But he worked real hard to improve. He caught batting practice every chance he got and took special practice on his greatest weakness, pop flies. He did have an excellent arm and he sure didn't have to work on his hitting very much. Nobody swung a better bat."

Gibson never did become a great defensive catcher. He had only average hands and never overcame his uncertainty on pop flies. Still, he improved to the point of being a very durable, strong-throwing, and efficient defensive catcher. According to Ted Page, Josh's catching reputation suffered because of jealousy. "It was just like Satchel," said Page. "People were jealous of Satchel's pitching ability, so they put him down, especially about his arrogant personality.

"Now with Josh, nobody could criticize his personality. He was just a big sweet overgrown boy who was a real joy to be around. Next to hitting, I think he liked eating ice cream more than anything else in the world. People criticized his catching ability because they wanted to bring him down to their level."

Emerging as a star, Josh smashed 75 round-trippers for the Grays in 1931. While his baseball life provided great happiness and satisfaction, tragedy struck off the field. Several years before, he had begun a romance with Helen Mason, a lovely girl from Pittsburgh's Hill District. Like the Gibsons, Helen's parents, James and Margaret, had moved North to escape the bigotry and extreme poverty of the deep South. Josh married Helen in 1930.

During August of 1931, the pregnant Helen went into complicated labor at Pittsburgh's Magee Hospital. She delivered twin babies, but the birth induced severe convulsions. She lapsed into a coma, and despite having the resilient strength of an eighteen-year-old, died of heart failure a few hours later. Just twenty himself, the devastated Josh faced the problem of raising Josh Jr. and Helen alone. Fortunately, since Josh traveled so much, his wife's family shouldered the major responsibility for raising the youngsters.

Following the 1931 season, Gus Greenlee began his serious raiding of the Homestead Grays. Gibson moved over to the Crawfords at the urging of Judy Johnson. Josh called Johnson "Jing," and the wise veteran had become his mentor in all aspects of baseball life.

Johnson and Gibson worked very well together on the field. Ted Page recalled an incident in 1932 that took advantage of Judy's intelligence and Josh's strong accurate arm. "The Crawfords were playing a team of major league All-Stars managed by Leo Durocher," said Page. "Durocher, as I'm sure everybody knows, was a big show-off, and when he made it to third base, he started dancing down the line to rattle our pitcher, Leroy Matlock. Then, I heard that little whistle which Judy gave to Josh when they were going to work a play. Judy went over to the mound and said loud enough for Durocher to hear, 'Wake up Leroy, this man's gonna steal the shirt right off your back.'

"Judy walked back and told Durocher, 'This guy's the dumbest pitcher we have on this team.' Then Judy repeated the little whistle. On the pitch, Durocher started heading down the line toward home and Judy went with him. But Judy went back and set himself up a couple of feet in front of the bag. Josh snapped the ball to Judy without even moving his feet. Durocher flew back into the bag, but the umpire called him out.

"Durocher argued, of course, but when Judy asked him to get off his foot, Leo knew he was done. His foot was right on Judy's ankle."

"Yes, Josh could throw," said Johnson, "but he could also run very well. That was one of the most overlooked parts of his game. He had excellent speed for a big guy and he was a very smart base runner. I don't ever remember seeing him make a base running mistake.

"I think Josh had the same problem as Babe Ruth in that everybody just saw him as a big power hitter. Josh could do a lot of things and so could Ruth. When Ruth was young, before he got his big belly, he could do it all. He was a great outfielder and he could run. Nobody had a better arm at that time, except maybe one of our guys, Martin Dihigo."

Despite his versatile skills, most remember Gibson's big bat. His exploits have become the stuff of legend. Jack Marshall, who spent most of his career with the Chicago American Giants, remembered one of Josh's drives at Chicago's Comiskey Park. According to Marshall, "The center-field fence at Comiskey Park was 435 feet from home plate. The wall was low and on top of it was a loudspeaker about 20 inches in diameter. Josh hit a line drive to center field that didn't seem to rise. It went like a frozen rope right smack into the middle of the loudspeaker. It stuck there and a groundskeeper had to pry it out."

Marshall also witnessed another of Gibson's remarkable feats, this time at Victory Field in Indianapolis, Indiana. "Sonny Cornelius was pitching for the American Giants," he said. "Sonny threw Josh a big slow curve and fooled him. Josh took his short stride, shifted his weight, and went into his swing. His left arm was already across his body when he recognized the slow curve. He took his left hand off the bat and just swatted the ball with his right hand. The ball still cleared the fence at about 375 feet.''

Besides the day his awesome drive almost cleared the triple deck at Yankee Stadium, Gibson had several other big days in ''the house that Ruth built.'' Bill Yancey, a shortstop with the New York Black Yankees, recalled one of those performances. ''Josh hit three homers that day and one of them was the quickest home run I ever saw. It was one of those line drives like Lou Gehrig used to hit and it left the park so fast that you couldn't turn your head quick enough to see it.''

''Another of the things I remember about Josh's hitting,'' says Cool Papa Bell, ''was the way he hit to all fields. He wasn't really a pull hitter. He hit the ball where it was pitched. I remember when we were playing down in the Dominican Republic and some of their boys came to Josh for some hitting advice during batting practice one day. Josh told them that it was important to hit the ball where it was pitched and hit to all fields. He then asked the batting practice pitcher to throw him three pitches, one outside, one inside, and one down the middle. He hit the outside pitch over the right field fence, the inside ball over the left field fence, and the one down the middle over the center-field fence. I don't think anybody could ever give a better exhibition of hitting.''

Gibson hit the ball far and he also hit it very hard. Ted Page remembered one of Josh's short line drives. ''I believe the Crawfords were playing in York, Pennsylvania,'' said Page. ''Josh hit a blistering liner right at Willie Wells. Now, Wells was a great shortstop, but he couldn't do anything with that ball. It hit his glove so hard it split the skin on the palm of his left hand. Remember, that was a tough hand, callused by catching a lot of balls.''

Despite Gibson's greatness, there were always those who thought they could handle him. Jimmie Crutchfield remembers such an occasion in a game between the Crawfords and the Nashville Elite Giants. ''There was a big crowd in Nashville that day,'' he says, ''including an entire minor league team that had come to see us play. Before the game, Candy Jim Taylor, the Elite Giants' manager, said he knew how to pitch Josh. He said Josh couldn't hit a sidearm pitch thrown by way of third base. Late in the game, we trailed by two runs. Cool Papa doubled and I drove him home with a single. Josh came up as the go-ahead run. Taylor went out to the mound and told his pitcher, Andrew Porter, to throw nothing but sidearm curves. Well, Porter came in with the sidewinder and Josh smashed it right out of the park on a line. As Josh went around the bases, he kind of chuckled and I heard him say, 'Ol Josh hit another one.' ''

Theodore "Highpockets" Trent, who owned an assortment of wicked curves, was one person who had some success against Josh. Trent had success against almost everyone, however, including Bill Terry, the National League's last .400 hitter, whom he fanned four times in one game. Another time, Trent struck out Rogers Hornsby, who once hit .424, three times in a row.

The stories abound, but Gibson, like the other Negro League players, suffered from the lack of careful statistics. "In 1933," says Cool Papa Bell, "they say I stole 175 bases. I stole a whole lot more than that, but sometimes they didn't even keep the book. People ask me how many homers Josh Gibson hit and I can't tell them for sure. I did count 72 in 1933. Josh and I played together on the Crawfords from 1933 through 1936, and during those seasons, I can tell you for sure that he never hit less than 60 home runs and maybe as many as 80 or 85."

Even Josh became expendable in 1937, when Gus Greenlee's racket money began to dry up. Greenlee traded Gibson, black baseball's greatest slugger, and Judy Johnson, its best third baseman, to Posey's Homestead Grays for catcher Pepper Bassett, infielder Harry Spearman, and $2,500. Insulted, Johnson retired. Along with many of his Crawford teammates, Josh went to play in the Dominican Republic. Late in July, following the Dominican Season, he reported to the Grays.

When he joined the Grays, Josh teamed with left-handed hitting first baseman Buck Leonard to form the most feared batting combination in black baseball. Like Gibson, Leonard could hit for both average and power. Also like Gibson, he was one of the first of the old black stars to be elected to the Baseball Hall of Fame.

Gibson hit third and Leonard fourth. Soon, reporters began to call the duo the "Black Babe Ruth" and the "Black Lou Gehrig." Many, including Jimmie Foxx, believed they were legitimately comparable to the great Yankee stars. According to Foxx, "You could have put Gibson and Leonard in the number three and four spots for the Yankees and nobody would have noticed the difference, except for maybe the skin color. They sure wouldn't have seen a difference with the bat."

Leonard remembers one of the first games in which he teamed with Gibson. "We were trailing the Newark Eagles 2–1," he says, "and they had Leon Day on the mound. Day was definitely one of the toughest pitchers in our league. We got a runner on first with nobody out, and the manager gave me the bunt sign. It was one of the few times in my career that I was asked to bunt, but I got the man down. Day really bore down and got two quick strikes on Josh. But Josh didn't seem to mind having two strikes at all. He didn't shorten his grip or widen his stance. Day put a tough curve ball right on the outside corner knee high and Josh nailed it over the scoreboard in dead center field. That man was some kind of hitter."

Josh Gibson, the Black Bomber.

Gibson hit 11 home runs in Washington's Griffith Stadium during 1943, and one day, Clark Griffith, owner of the destitute Washington Senators, called him and Buck Leonard to his office. "We thought he was going to offer us contracts with the Senators," recalls Leonard. "But all he said was that it would cause a lot of trouble if he took us into the major leagues. Later, I heard he told somebody that integration would ruin Negro baseball and spoil his business relationship with the Grays."

After two excellent seasons with the Grays, Gibson jumped to Vera Cruz of the Mexican League. The Grays offered him $500 a month for the summer season, but the Mexicans offered him $800 a month for eight months, more than some major league contracts.

Besides the money, Josh enjoyed playing in Latin America. His name had become legend in Puerto Rico, his home for winter ball since 1933. In San Juan, a ring of palm trees, some 50 feet behind the fence, surrounded the walls of Escambron Stadium. Many times over the years, despite the heavy tropical air, Josh powered drives into these trees, a distance of some 500 feet from home plate. A daring worker attached a bright marker to each spot in the trees where one of the blasts disappeared. The markers remained in place for many years, a tribute to Gibson's awesome power. The Puerto Rican fans also placed a stone monument honoring Josh in center field. The monument is similar to those erected for Babe Ruth and Lou Gehrig in Yankee Stadium.

Josh also enjoyed Puerto Rico because he could spend many hours discussing baseball with his good friend Perucho Cepeda, the island's native baseball hero. Gibson had known Cepeda for years and they had played together in Puerto Rico as well as played for Rafael Trujillo in the Dominican Republic. Cepeda, a muscular shortstop, was known as "El Toro," or "The Bull," because of his considerable long distance power. Perucho's son, Orlando, often listened to their stories and to their advice. He later became known as "The Baby Bull" during his fine major league career.

Josh considered his accomplishments in Puerto Rico very important. Following the 1941 season, he received trophies for being both the Puerto Rican League's batting champion and most valuable player. The honors were quite meaningful to Josh because black baseball gave no such awards.

At Vera Cruz, Josh also terrorized Mexican League pitchers. In 1941, for instance, he hit .345 and led the league in homers with 33 and RBI's with 124. It was to be his last great show.

Gibson rejoined the Grays in 1942 and began a long and painful slide to oblivion. In Latin America, Josh's great taste for vanilla ice cream had changed to a great taste for beer, and his sometimes excessive drinking contributed to his downfall. Once an iron 200 pounds, his weight climbed to 230, which along with cartilage damage to his knees from so many games behind the plate, led to his almost continuous fatigue.

Soon, even more ominous factors surfaced. Josh suffered many dizzy spells and on pop flies, always a problem for him, he often became entirely disoriented. Buck Leonard and Howard Easterling, a third baseman, tried to help Josh by catching every pop-up within their reach.

The Grays met the Kansas City Monarchs in the 1942 Negro League World Series, but lost in four straight. Josh hit only .200, a major factor in the Grays' defeat. His doctor advised him to stay at home and rest instead of playing his usual winter season in Puerto Rico. Gibson followed some of the advice by remaining in Pittsburgh. He rested little. Despite increasingly frequent headaches, Josh continued to drink and enjoy the good life at the Crawford Grille. During the afternoon of New Year's Day, 1943, following a rousing celebration the night and early morning before, Gibson lost consciousness and lapsed into a coma. He was admitted to Pittsburgh's St. Francis Hospital, where he revived several hours later. When he was released after only ten days, the doctors were evasive. They reported only that "Mr. Gibson had suffered a nervous breakdown."

The Grays' owner, Cum Posey, writing about Gibson in his "Posey's Paragraphs" column for the *Pittsburgh Courier* on January 23, said, "He was worried about his batting and overworked himself in an effort to hit his usual playing stride. He was ordered to take a long rest by his physician at the close of the season, but did not follow the doctor's orders until he was completely run down. He is now the same Josh who never knew the candle had two ends."

While the details of the illness remained sketchy, which aroused the suspicion of Posey and others, Josh refused to reveal the true danger of his condition. The doctors had diagnosed a brain tumor. Josh kept the diagnosis secret from all except his family and refused surgery, fearing it would leave him a vegetable.

Josh's hitting ability seemed little impaired, as he hit .503 for the 1943 season. His drinking bouts and episodes of erratic behavior continued to become more frequent, however. When drunk, he became loud and wild. He often roared into the Crawford Grille and demanded free drinks. He was quickly served, as nobody wanted to risk the violent anger of a man with such awesome strength. During one of these episodes at the Grille, Gibson became so rowdy that the police strapped him into a straightjacket while holding him at gunpoint. After the police had put their guns away, Josh ripped off the jacket with an enormous burst of strength, stared the officers down, and walked out into the street. Nobody dared to follow.

Another time, during the 1943 season, the Grays were resting between games of a day-night doubleheader at Carver Hall, a rooming house in Washington, D.C. Some of the players found Josh sitting alone by the window of his second-floor room and carrying on an imaginary conversation with Joe DiMaggio.

For the next three seasons, Josh continued to hit for a very high average, even leading the league with a .393 mark in 1945. The 1946 season proved to be especially painful. His damaged knees prevented him from playing much of the time, and when he did, it was with a noticeable limp. Two East-West games were played that season, and the fans voted Josh to both. In the first, at Griffith Stadium, he singled in his second time at bat and was removed for a pinch runner. In the second, at Comiskey Park, he failed to hit the ball out of the infield in three tries.

Jimmie Crutchfield visited Josh after the Chicago game. Earlier in the year, Crutchfield had seen Gibson drinking straight whiskey, shot after shot. Perhaps sensing impending tragedy, Jimmie asked his old friend for an autograph. "Hey, Jimmie," smiled Josh, "I should be asking for your autograph." The flattered Gibson signed Jimmie's small piece of paper, and he keeps it in a safe-deposit box to this day.

Josh fell deeper into despair at the end of the season. While living in his mother's home at 2410 Strauss on Pittsburgh's North Side, he drank heavily and continuously complained about headaches, dizziness, and the pain in his knees. Besides the possible brain tumor, Josh now suffered from hypertension. By the New Year of 1947, his weight had dropped to 180 pounds, which was quite frail for him.

Josh's health continued to worsen in January of that year, and his frequent headaches became almost unbearable. On the night of January 19, Josh came home and told his mother he felt very sick. Ted Page remembered Gibson's death as related to him by Annie Mahaffey, Josh's sister. " 'Josh told my mother he was going to have a stroke. She told him he wasn't going to have no stroke and put him to bed. We gathered around his bed and waited for the doctor. Josh was really in pretty good spirits. He sent his brother Jerry around to collect his trophies and his radio and bring them home. Jerry got back about 10:30. We were all sitting around Josh's bed talking and then he had a stroke. He just got through laughing and tried to say something, but you couldn't understand him. Then he just laid down and died.' "

According to another version, Josh's stroke occurred at the Garden Theater, a movie house. He remained unconscious, and failing to respond to medication, passed away at his mother's home during the early morning hours of January 20.

No matter the exact circumstances, Josh Gibson, the man with the big bat, and the big smile, was gone. The funeral was held at the Macedonia Baptist Church on Bedford Avenue, just a few steps from the sandlots where young Josh first impressed everyone with his marvelous hitting. Hundreds attended the services, marking it as one of the biggest funerals in Pittsburgh history.

Ted Page believed his friend died of a broken heart. "Josh knew he had great ability and he wanted to be the one to break the color barrier. When the Dodgers signed Jackie Robinson, he knew it was over for him. He wasn't going to make the big leagues, and he also knew that because of his health and his bad knees his career with the Grays was about over. He didn't know what to do with his life. He had no options.

"They say a man can't die of a broken heart, and I guess that's true. But, I'll tell you this, all of this sure lessened Josh's will to keep going, to keep fighting to stay alive."

Josh died almost penniless. Donations paid for most of the funeral. There wasn't enough money to pay for a gravestone. A small metal oval marked his grave. Allegheny County provided it.

6

Flying Feet

He is a beautiful person. Yes he is, Cool Papa Bell.
He is a lovable person. And always has been. I love
him. My goodness. That's one beautiful man.

Dave Barnhill, Pitcher
New York Cubans

*T*he lightning-quick James "Cool Papa" Bell, the Crawfords' center fielder, proved himself to be a deadly hitter, a superb flyhawk, and the swiftest runner in baseball's long history. Just how fast was Cool Papa? Well, listen to the master storyteller, Satchel Paige. "One day when I was pitchin' to Cool, he drilled one right through my legs and was hit in the back by his own ground ball when he slid into second."

How about this? Satchel again, "Bell was so fast that he could flip the switch and then jump in bed before the light went out." Paige amused audiences with his story for well over 40 years, but, of course, nobody really believed him.

Finally, at the 1981 Negro Baseball Reunion in Ashland, Kentucky, Cool Papa assured everyone that his old friend was telling the truth. "During one winter season in the late 1930s, Satchel and I roomed together out in California. One night, before he got back, I turned off the light, but it didn't go out right away. There was a delay of about three seconds between the time I flipped the switch and the time the light went out. There must of been a short or somethin'.

"I thought to myself, here's a chance to fool ol' Satch. He was always playin' tricks on everybody else you know. Anyway, when he came back to the room, I said, 'Hey, Satch, I'm pretty fast, right?' 'You're the fastest,' he said.

"Well, you haven't seen nothin' yet,' I told him. 'Why, I'm so fast, I can turn out the light and be in bed before the room gets dark.' 'Sure, Cool. Sure you can,' he said.

"I told him to sit down an' watch. I turned off the light, jumped in bed, and pulled the covers up to my chin. Then the light went out.

"I howled and Satchel was speechless for once. Anyway, he's been tellin' the truth all these years."

Although no mythical Paul Bunyon or Pecos Bill, Bell did possess truly amazing speed. The Crawfords' third baseman, Judy Johnson, remembered the first time he played against Cool. "I saw him down in Cuba one winter during the 1920s. He was so fast that if he hit a groundball to the left side of the infield that took more than one hop, you just couldn't throw him out. Might just as well hold the ball. When he came around second with a full head of steam, it looked like his feet weren't even touching the ground. Believe it or not, he'd steal second standing up and he'd sometimes score from first on a single or from second on a deep fly ball."

Cool Papa Bell in 1928.

Despite his awesome talent, Cool Papa is most remembered by his teammates as a marvelous human being. Ted Page, who played alongside Bell and Jimmie Crutchfield in the legendary Crawfords' outfield, said, "Most people think about speed when they talk about Cool, and he certainly was fast. We used to kid 'im about having wings on his feet and tell 'im to jump off buildings. I'll tell you this, though, he was an even better man off the field than he was on it. He was honest. He was kind. He was a clean liver. In fact, in all the years I've known him, I've never seen him smoke, take a drink, or say even one cuss word."

Born in Starkville, Mississippi, on May 17, 1903, James Bell learned about life from his mother, Mae. He remembers her with tears in his eyes. "My mother always told me that it didn't make any difference about the color of my skin, or how much money I had. The only thing that counted was to be an honest, clean livin' man who cared about other people. I've always tried to live up to those words."

Bell first played baseball in the hot dusty fields around Starkville. Barefooted, with only homemade equipment, he often joined in the wonderful games which always lasted until dark.

He tasted real baseball glory for the first time during his tenth summer and he cherishes the memory. "Even though I was just a little boy, I could throw hard. My older sister, Bessie, had also shown me how to throw a knuckleball. One day there was a picnic in a community called Blackjack. After the picnic, the men played a game and they asked me to pitch. I was scared, but I went out and did my best. I pitched three innings and struck out eight of the nine men I faced. The only man who hit the ball was Joe Miner. He was the best hitter around, a big guy with thick wrists and real strong forearms. But all he could do was hit a little grounder back to me.

"When it was my turn to hit, a big woman came running to the plate, picked me up, and put me on her shoulders. She yelled at the pitcher, 'You're throwin' the ball too fast, and this little boy's gonna get hurt.' But they convinced her to let me bat, and on the first pitch, I hit a line drive into the outfield for a single. Oooee, was I happy.

"After the game, the girls came running up to me and gave me a big piece of chocolate cake. I remember that game better than any I ever played as a professional."

In August of 1920, Bell moved to St. Louis seeking a better job than could be found in Starkville. He found work at the Independent Meat Packing Company and also joined the all-black Compton Hill Cubs of the St. Louis City League. He soon established a fine reputation as a left-handed pitcher, even though his manager wouldn't let him throw his darting knuckleball. Nobody, except his sister Bessie, could handle the elusive butterfly without suffering damaged fingers.

The Cubs disbanded after the 1921 season and the following spring, May 3, 1922, Bell signed his first professional contract. For $90 a month, he sold his pitching talent to the St. Louis Stars of the powerful Negro National League. The Stars played their home games at Dick Kent's ballyard, named after the team's owner, a prominent operator in the St. Louis underworld. The field spread next to the old streetcar barns and was surrounded by sun-bleached wooden stands and a rickety fence which seemed ready to fall down because of the many peepholes drilled through it.

Bell's first big pitching test came in Chicago against the best team in black baseball, Rube Foster's splendid American Giants. In addition to their great speed, the American Giants' lineup included the great Cuban star, Cristobal Torriente, one of the premier sluggers in black baseball.

Backed by a large noisy crowd at Asbury Park, the American Giants applied intense pressure on newcomer Bell in the very first inning. The first three men in their lineup, all speedburners, Jelly Gardner, Bingo DeMoss, and David Malarcher, bunted. In James Bell, however, (much to their surprise) they had challenged a man even quicker than themselves. Moving with cat-like grace, Bell glided from sideline to sideline, scooped up the bunts, and punched the runners out at first.

The American Giants did manage to put three runs on the board, however, and in the bottom of the fifth, they had the go-ahead run on second with two outs and the great Cristobal Torriente at the plate. The screaming crowd did its best to break Bell's composure, but using his fastball, and nibbling at the outside corner with his curve, he worked the count to two and two. He then served up one of his floating butterflies and the surprised Torriente fanned for the third out. Bell remembers the pitch: "My knuckleball had a good break, but I couldn't control it very well, so I didn't throw it often. I also threw it slow so it worked as a change-up. I just kept shakin' off my catcher, Sam Bennett, until the knuckler was the only pitch left. It was the first one I threw that day, so Torriente was completely fooled."

"Hey, kid," called Bennett as they returned to the bench, "you're mighty cool out there."

"Yeah, cool," agreed pitcher Jimmy Oldham. "Let's call 'im Cool."

Manager Bill Gatewood said, "Ya know, Cool's not really enough, he needs more of a name. How about Cool Papa?" Everyone agreed, and like two other left-handed pitchers who converted to the outfield, Babe Ruth and Stan Musial, it was Cool Papa all the way to the Hall of Fame.

Cool pitched the Stars to a 4–3 victory over the American Giants that prophetic day and even drove home the winning run with a perfect squeeze bunt. As he headed for the dressing room, Foster called, "Hey, Bell, c'mon over here for a minute." Offering congratulations, the big man crushed Cool Papa's hand with his iron grip. "You did real fine today," he said. "You move good. I'd like to see just how fast you really are. "C'mere, Jimmy," he called to the American Giants' bench.

The fleet Jimmy Lyons, whom most considered the fastest man in the league, stood up and ambled over. "Jimmy," said Foster, "I want you and Bell here to have a little race."

"Sure," said Lyons as he eyed the streamlined Bell. Cool hesitated a moment and then nodded in agreement. As their teammates gathered around the two greyhounds, Foster stepped off 100 yards from home plate down the right field line.

Bell lined up in a slightly crouched position. Lyons, an experienced racer, assumed the classic sprinter's stance. On Rube's signal, the two men powered into motion. Lyons boomed away and led in the early going. Then Cool Papa, his long legs stretching and reaching, roared past him and cruised to an easy victory amidst the whoops and yells of the St. Louis team.

Cool remembers two things about Rube Foster that day. One was his grip. "I've shaken hands with some strong men, including Oscar Charleston, Josh Gibson, and Willie Mays," he says, "but Rube Foster's grip was definitely the strongest of them all."

Second, Cool remembers Foster's reaction to his victory in the race. "He came over to me and said, 'Son, I didn't think anybody could beat Lyons and you beat 'im a long way.' He didn't like my baseball shoes very much though. They only cost $1, but it was the best I could do then. He said, 'If you can run that well in those shoes, just think what you might do in a good pair. Tell you what, go down to the Spalding Sporting Goods Store and tell the man you want the best pair of spikes he has in stock. Charge 'em to me.'

"I said, thanks very much, Mr. Foster. I'll get the shoes, but I'm going to pay you for them. I was raised to pay my debts. The man at the store gave me a pair of kangaroo-hide baseball shoes. They cost $21, but by the end of the season, I had saved enough to pay Mr. Foster back."

The next week, Foster offered Dick Kent seven players for Bell, but was turned down. Although disappointed, Rube remained Cool's friend and mentor over the next few years, always ready to share his immense wisdom about baseball and about life.

After the 1922 season, Cool played against his first major league competition when the Stars met the Detroit Tigers in a three-game series. The Stars won two of three, but future Hall-of-Famers Ty Cobb and Harry Heilmann refused to play for Detroit. Cobb was keeping the promise he made in Havana 12 years earlier when he had been humiliated by John Henry Lloyd and Bruce Petway.

"You know," says Cool, "the baseball commissioner, Judge Landis, didn't want the whites to play against black teams because we won too often. He told the white boys they couldn't wear their major league uniforms when they played us, and they had to call themselves All-Stars. He even wanted them to play under assumed names. Some of the boys, like Dizzy Dean, Jimmie Foxx, and the Waner brothers, didn't pay any attention to him. They were real friendly to us. Guys like Lefty Grove and Al Simmons weren't so friendly."

During spring training in 1924, St. Louis club officials put a stopwatch on their speedster. Bell raced from home to first in 3.1 seconds and covered the entire circuit in an astonishing 12 seconds flat. By contrast, Evar Swanson of the Cincinnati Reds holds the major league mark for circling the bases at 13.3 seconds.

The Stars' management decided to convert Bell into an outfielder and teach him to switch hit. Until then, he had been a right-handed batter. "It took me almost two years to get comfortable hitting from the left," Cool remembers. "In fact, for a long time, when I got two strikes on the left side, I switched back to the right."

Still, becoming an outfielder allowed Bell to emerge as one of the most sensational players in black baseball. Over the next few years, he consistently hit in the .300s, with a .340 mark in 1926, .359 in 1929, and .377 in 1930. During his 10 years with the Stars, Cool led the team to three NNL championships and also victimized many major leaguers with his flying feet. In 1931, for instance, a talented group of barnstorming big leaguers swashbuckled into St. Louis to meet the Stars. They were led by Max Carey, "Big Poison" Paul Waner, and "Little Poison" Lloyd Waner, all of whom wound up in the Hall of Fame. Cool and his men whipped them into full retreat with an 18–3 pasting.

Bell set the tone of the game in his first at bat with a perfectly placed bunt for a hit. He swiped second and third on the next two pitches. Then, with tension high, he danced off third, a running start . . . stop . . . another false start . . . a nervous Bill Walker delivering the pitch . . . a black gazelle driving down the line and sliding safely home in a cloud of dust.

"Lloyd Waner never forgot that game," Bell remembers. "A few years later, when I was in Pittsburgh, Waner used to come in the Crawford Grille when the Pirates were in town. He told me that after that game one of the other white boys said, 'Bell is like a black Ty Cobb.' But Waner said he told him, 'You're wrong. Cobb is like a white Bell.' "

How might Cool Papa have fared if allowed to play in the big leagues? Well, in 46 games against major league competition, batting against such men as Dizzy Dean, Bob Feller, Johnny VanderMeer, Bob Lemon, Murry Dickson, and Johnny Allen, off whom he hit three homers in one game, Bell ripped the ball at a .395 clip. He also stole bases almost at will. Today, even at age 88, Bell stands tall and erect. Had he played in the major leagues, one suspects he might be somewhat stooped from carrying his money to the bank.

Sometimes, however, those in authority used their power to keep the blacks in their place. In 1935, in a game against the Dizzy Dean All-Stars, Bell tasted some of this medicine. "The Crawfords were playing in Yankee Stadium," he says. "I was on second after hitting a double off Diz and Josh Gibson came up. Now, Josh had hit some real long balls off Dean. Diz turned to his outfield and started yelling, 'Get back, get back.' Jimmy Ripple, who was playing center field, said, 'How far do you want me to go back?' Diz said, 'Just go back as far as you can.' Gibson hit a deep fly to Ripple. I tagged up and headed for third. Dick Lundy, the third base coach, put on the stop sign. But I noticed that the shortstop was just getting the ball from Ripple. It was a scoreless tie, so I decided to gamble. The ball came in high to the catcher and I slid right under him. He never did tag me, but the umpire called me out. I said, 'I was safe,' but he said, 'Maybe you can score from second on an outfield fly in your league, but I'm not going to let you get away with it against major leaguers.' Some people came down out of the stands after the umpire. One of them had a knife and I almost got cut. Dean's team won anyway when Ray Dandridge made a wild throw in the next inning."

Cool Papa joined the Crawfords in 1933 and he was glad to have a job. "I needed work," he says. "I had some rough times after the St. Louis Stars went out of business." So, when Greenlee called I went right to Pittsburgh to see him. He even paid my expenses.

"Even though I needed the job, I was a little cautious about Greenlee because I knew of his gangster reputation. I knew about gangsters, because our owner in St. Louis, Dick Kent, was that kind. Still, I wish I could have asked Rube Foster about Greenlee. But that wasn't possible.

"When I got there, Greenlee won me over right away. He was a very nice man. He told me I had a chance to be part of the best team in the history of black baseball and that I was the key. He needed a good center fielder to make a good team a great team. I told him I hoped I could do the job for him."

Bell certainly did the job. He combined with Satchel Paige and Josh Gibson to give Greenlee the three most exciting players in black baseball. Even among this elite company, Bell's star shone the brightest in 1933, as he stole 175 bases, while hitting .379 with 63 doubles, 17 triples, and 11 home runs.

Fans everywhere flocked to see the sleek black panther who roamed center field for the Crawfords. They came to see him hit, and they came to see him throw, but mostly they came to marvel at the magic of his flying feet. Nothing delighted his admirers more than to share the excitement as he blurred on the basepaths or raced across the outfield greenery to make a spectacular catch.

Bell enjoyed playing in Pittsburgh as much as the fans appreciated having him there. "In St. Louis," he says, "we played on a pretty bad field. Very little grass but lots of junk. The fence was about to fall down so were the bleachers. It didn't seem much better than playing in the fields back in Mississippi.

"Greenlee Field was a whole different story. It was beautiful. It had lots of grass and you almost felt like you were playing in a major league park. The best thing for me was the big outfield. It gave me lots of room to run.

"Gus really did his best to run a class organization. We had a fine bus, nice uniforms, good equipment, everything. I think he could have paid us more, but it just didn't work out that way.

"I really appreciated the fans in Pittsburgh, too. Along with the fans in St. Louis, they were the best I saw during my career. Most of them seemed to really appreciate our efforts."

Still, even the exciting Crawfords needed special attractions to keep the fans happy and survive during the hard financial times of the Great Depression. Late in the 1936 season, Jesse Owens traveled with the club. Fresh from the summer Olympic Games in Berlin where he had humiliated Adolph Hitler and his Nazi supremacists by winning four gold medals, Owens fattened attendance by running exhibition races before the games.

In a carnival atmosphere, Jesse pitted his speed against both men and horses. In San Antonio, for example, one man started at home, another at first, one at second, and still another at third. Each man raced one base against Owens. Before they could gain momentum, Jesse streaked past them at full speed as the crowd roared its approval.

Owens also did well against the horses. Being slow starters, Jesse always beat the animals at 60 yards. Once, however, he made the mistake of racing a quarter horse. Jesse fired out to his usual quick start and so did the horse. Much to his embarrassment, it blazed past him to win.

In 100-yard dashes, Owens gave his opponent a 15-yard head start. When he raced Speed Whatley, the Crawfords' young burner, Jesse should have been given the head start. Whatley widened the gap as he won the race.

Many of the Crawfords wanted Bell to race Owens, but manager Oscar Charleston said to Cool, "You can beat Whatley, so I know you can beat Owens. I know you won't let him beat you, so I won't let you race. We need him as a gate attraction."

In Cleveland, Charleston yielded to pressure and gave permission for the race. Jesse refused. "I don't want to run today," he said. "I didn't bring my track shoes."

Several of the Crawfords gave Owens a real hard time about refusing to race, but Cool Papa urged them to ease off. He said, "Let him be. Do you think he enjoys playing the clown? He's just tryin' to make a living for himself and his family. He was promised movies and all kinds of endorsements but they backed away because he was black. It's very important for him to keep his reputation."

In 1937, Bell played for Rafael Trujillo in the Dominican Republic and the next year moved to Mexico. It was there that he learned of the death of his mother Mae back in Mississippi. She, along with his wife, Clara, had been the light of his life. From 1919, when he went to work in St. Louis, until the time of her death, he sent money home to her. Despite some very rough financial times for himself, he didn't miss a week in nearly 20 years. Why? "Because she was my mother," he says.

Jesse Owens

Bell played only four years for the Crawfords, but the times remain among his most cherished memories. "I wish it could have lasted longer," he says. "We had such a great team, a team that could win games in every way possible. Charleston was not a great teacher, except by example, but I thought he was a very good manager.

"Charleston was a complete ballplayer in that he could hit, hit for power, run, throw, and field. He realized the importance of all of these things and managed accordingly. He didn't mind winning with the long ball, but on the whole he managed more like Rube Foster. He played for Foster at one time you know, and he learned the importance of fundamentals. He liked to use the hit-and-run, the bunt-and-run, the run-and-bunt, the squeeze, and all those tricky plays. Charleston was a master of tricky baseball and I liked that. I was sorry I had to leave the Crawfords."

From 1938 through 1941, Bell played in Mexico where postcards depicted him as "The Great Batter of the Mexican League." Great indeed, especially at Torreon in 1940 when he led the league in hitting with a .437 average and slammed 20 homers. "Funny thing about those homers," Bell says. "The record shows I only hit 12, but I really had 20. Eight of them were inside the park, so they would only give me credit for doubles. They said I was too fast and it wasn't fair to give me home runs. Now, down in Cuba, I was the first man to hit three homers in one game. They came off Johnny Allen, who went on to the Yankees, and they were all over the fence."

While Cool Papa won the Mexican League batting championship, he lost another the same year under unusual circumstances. Playing in Cuba during the winter season, he led the league at .360 with only six games left to play. The closest man trailed by many points. When Bell's team fell out of championship contention, the management sent him and four other Americans home early without final pay. Cool would have collected $500 for winning the batting title, but since he left early, the league officials claimed he didn't deserve the championship or the money.

Cool played for the Chicago American Giants in 1942 and then joined the Homestead Grays in 1943. He put together four excellent years for the Grays, hitting .327 in 1943, .373 in 1944, .302 in 1945, and .411 in 1946. The .373 average in 1944 should have meant another batting title, but with Cool's permission, league officials manipulated the figures to allow the Philadelphia Stars' shortstop Frank Austin to win. Again, in 1946, Cool's .411 led the league, but once more with his permission, the league used a technicality to declare Monte Irvin the champion with a .394 average.

Satchel Paige explained why Cool relinquished these two batting championships. "Cool Papa? The man had no selfishness or jealousy in him. He knew he was too old to do a job in the majors and he knew it was important for our boys to do a good job when they got the chance. He let Austin and Irvin win because he thought they had a good chance to make the majors. He was right about Irvin."

Cool had his last hurrah in Los Angeles on October 24, 1948, while playing for Satchel Paige's Royal All-Stars against a group of major leaguers led by Cleveland pitcher, and future Hall-of-Famer, Bob Lemon. Ironically, Jackie Robinson played second base for the Lemon team that day.

In an interview given shortly before his death in 1989, Murry Dickson, who pitched the last four innings for the Lemon Stars, described Cool Papa's flying feet. "Before the game, I heard Satchel kidding Bob Lemon about this old guy who was going to show us up. His name was Cool Papa Bell.

"Lemon was not about to be intimidated by anyone, so the first time Bell came up, he put one right under his chin and knocked him down. The old boy got right up and hit the next pitch for a double. As soon as he got on base, he got a real big jump and stole third base standing up. Lemon was really mad.

"I relieved Lemon in the sixth inning, and Bell hit one right through my legs into center field for a single. The next batter popped up and then for some strange reason, Satchel decided to bunt. We had a big lead, but he decided to bunt anyway. He probably wanted to make sure he didn't have to run the bases. He pushed a nice bunt down the third baseline. Bell broke with the pitch, and the third baseman saw he couldn't get him at second, so he threw Satchel out at first.

"Bell came around second and saw nobody was covering third. Maybe the shortstop should'a been there or maybe I should'a been there, but we weren't. When Bell saw that open base, you should'a seen him light out. The third baseman tried to get back to the bag and the catcher, Roy Partee, also ran down to try and cover. This left home plate open. I guess I was asleep again. Bell just kept going and scored with no problem. Partee tried to call time out, but the ball was in play. When somebody scores from first base on a bunt, I guess you can say he showed you up."

After finishing his playing career with the Detroit Wolverines in 1947, Bell managed the Kansas City Stars, a farm club of the Kansas City Monarchs, from 1948 through 1951. He played a major role in the development of many young players, including Yankee standout Elston Howard and shortstop Ernie Banks, who now sits with the elite in Cooperstown. He had been promised one-third of the selling price when the Monarchs sold a player to the major leagues, but when Banks was sold to the Chicago Cubs for $30,000, greed prevailed. Instead of $10,000, Cool received a basket of fruit. A basket of fruit!

Following the 1951 season, as the black leagues agonized in their death throes, the man with flying feet ran off the field for the last time. His winter had begun, and Cool Papa Bell went home to St. Louis for good.

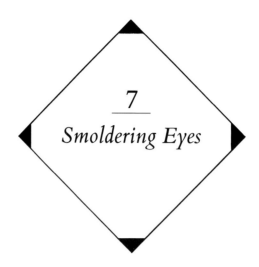

7

Smoldering Eyes

---

*It's impossible for anybody to be a better ball player
than Oscar Charleston.*

Grantland Rice

If only I could calcimine him.

John McGraw, Hall of Fame Manager
New York Giants

---

*W*hen the old black ball players discuss who was the best among them, they mention Satchel Paige, Joe Williams, Josh Gibson, Cool Papa Bell, and others. But only two names receive real consideration, Martin Dihigo and Oscar Charleston.

"Martin Dihigo was a marvelous athlete and a marvelous player," said Judy Johnson. "He could play every position well, including pitcher. He had the best arm I've ever saw. The only one close to his arm was Roberto Clemente. But as great as Dihigo was, there is no question in my mind that Oscar Charleston was the best player I ever saw, black or white."

Cool Papa Bell agrees with Johnson. "Now some could do certain things better than Charleston. For instance, I could run faster. Josh Gibson could hit the ball harder. But as an all-around player he was the best. He could hit for average and he could hit for power. He loved to hit in clutch situations and he was the guy you wanted up there.

"He played real shallow in the outfield like Willie Mays. But Mays let too many balls get over his head. Charleston caught everything.

"As I said, I was faster than Charleston, but not much. He could really run, and he was the smartest and most aggressive baserunner I ever saw. You talk about comin' in with spikes high or runnin' over a catcher. You shoulda' seen Charleston. He was as tough as they come."

Everybody remembered Charleston's leonine eyes, smoldering with mystery and secret fury. "He had cold gray eyes with a tint of blue," said Ted Page. "Vicious eyes. Like a cat. I remember reading once that all the great gunfighters of the Old West, guys like Wild Bill Hickok and Wyatt Earp, had those same blue-gray eyes. Well, I can tell you for sure that Charley would have made a helluva gunfighter."

Others remember his strength. "One time when we were with the Grays," said Judy Johnson, "Charleston was driving a bunch of us. The car went out of control and rolled over several times. Luckily, we were all thrown clear, and nobody got hurt. We found Charleston in the ditch with the steering wheel in his hands. He just ripped it right off when we crashed."

The man with smoldering eyes feared nobody. "Once," says Cool Papa Bell, "we were playing someplace in the South, Florida I think. After the game, we came out and some of the Ku Klux Klan tried to stop us. They had those hoods on their heads. Everybody was kinda' scared, except for Charleston. He just walked up and ripped the hood right off one of those guys. After that, none of them tried to mess with us.

Oscar Charleston in 1935.

"Another time, on a train, Charleston and some of the boys were fooling around and making a lot of noise. This big guy told them to shut up. Charleston went and stood over the big guy and said, "No, you shut up, or I'll throw you out the window. Somebody said to Charleston, 'Don't you know that's Jim Londos, the heavyweight wrestler? Charleston gave Londos a cold stare and said, 'I don't care who it is.' Londos never said another word."

Oscar learned his toughness on the streets of Indianapolis, where he was born on October 12, 1896, the seventh of eleven children born to Tom and Mary Charleston. He showed great interest in baseball as a youngster and became the batboy for the local black professional club, the ABCs. Sometimes, the manager allowed him to work out with the team, and though only in his early teens, Oscar held his own with the men.

A certain restlessness also lay behind the smoldering eyes, and when he was just fifteen years old, Charleston ran away from home and joined the army. He served in the Philippines with the all-black 24th infantry regiment, running on the track team and playing baseball. Charleston returned to Indianapolis with a tough mind and a rock-hard body. His hands, wrists, and forearms were especially powerful, all important assets for a baseball player.

Charleston signed to play with the Indianapolis ABCs in 1915 for $50 a month. That fall, following a successful rookie season, he faced white major league competition for the first time when the ABCs played a group of barnstormers managed by Donie Bush, the former Detroit Tigers' shortstop.

Charleston's temper, which would become legendary, erupted during the final game of the series. A close call went against the ABCs, and second baseman Bingo DeMoss launched a tirade. When umpire Jimmy Scanlon shoved DeMoss, Charleston came in from center field on the dead run and knocked the official cold.

Fans poured out of the stands and the police barely managed to prevent a full-scale riot. Both DeMoss and Charleston were arrested. Later they jumped bail and quietly left town for the Cuban winter season.

According to Ted Page, Charleston loved to fight as much as he loved to play baseball. "Charley was always ready to fight. He didn't smoke. He didn't drink. But he enjoyed a good fight. You know, fighting was common in Negro baseball. When there was a fight, and I was on the opposing team, I made sure I knew where Charleston was. I wanted no part of him. I wasn't the only one. Mule Suttles, Jud Wilson, John Beckwith, Dick Redding, none of those big strong guys wanted to mess with him either. Everybody except Josh Gibson was afraid of him.

"One time down in Cuba, Charley tried to stretch a long single into a double and the ball got to second base the same time he did. Well, of course, Charleston knocked the little shortstop into left field. This shortstop had guts. He came running back looking for a fight. Charleston knocked him down and out with one punch and then did the same to the second baseman. A whole bunch of soldiers came out of the stands and went after him. He laid them out all over the park. And he loved it. He had a big grin on his face all the time."

Once in Cuba, however, the police saved Charleston. He made a spectacular catch by reaching over the fence in deepest center field. When a fan pulled the ball out of his glove, Charleston picked the man up with one hand, deposited him on the field, and began working him over. Several of the man's friends jumped over the fence and attacked Oscar with their machetes. Fearless as always,

Oscar Charleston, Josh Gibson, Ted Page, and
Judy Johnson in 1932.

Charleston began bobbing and weaving, trying to get his powerful hands on the
men. One of the rescuing policeman took a medal from his own uniform and
pinned it on Charleston's chest. "You're a brave man," he said.

While intimidating the opposition with his physical presence at 5'11" and a
muscular 200 pounds, Charleston also needled them with his showboating in the
outfield. Sometimes he would start late for a flyball so a last-second burst of speed
was needed to make the catch. He often caught easy flies behind his back, on his
hip, or at the shoetops. Cool Papa Bell remembers him turning a somersault or a
back flip while a ball was in the air and still catching it. Charleston accomplished
all of this with a very small glove, common for his time.

Despite his fighting and his showboating, Charleston was an intense competitor who played very serious baseball. After five years with the ABCs, and one
with the Chicago American Giants, he moved to the St. Louis Giants in 1921.
There he put together perhaps his greatest season. Playing a 60-game schedule,
he ripped the ball at a .434 clip with 12 doubles, 15 home runs, and 34 stolen
bases.

During his younger days, Charleston used his great speed to steal bases almost
at will. As he grew older, he continued to steal almost anytime he wanted as his
baseball intelligence compensated for his lack of footspeed. Jimmie Crutchfield
says, "Charleston was a great ballplayer, but he was no teacher. You had to watch
him to learn. When I played for him on the Crawfords, he was already old and

fat. It was hard fat, but it was fat and he couldn't run very well. Still, he stole a lot of bases, especially in key situations where we really needed one. He did it by getting a great jump, by knowing what pitch to run on, and by using his great sliding ability to avoid the tags. I learned a lot by watching him."

During the fall following his great season with the St. Louis Giants, Charleston and his teammates met the National League's St. Louis Cardinals in a three-game series. The Cardinals were already aware of Charleston, because in 1917, he had slammed a long home run off the great Walter Johnson to give Smokey Joe Williams a 1–0 victory. The Cardinals managed to win two of the three despite the absence of NL batting champion Rogers Hornsby, who on this particular occasion refused to play against blacks. Charleston lived up to his reputation, however, when his long shot to their right field pavilion roof keyed the Giants' 5–4 win in the first game.

Records indicate that in 53 games against major league competition, Charleston hit .318 with 11 homers. According to Dizzy Dean, "Charleston could hit the ball a mile. He didn't have a weakness. When he came up, we just threw and hoped he wouldn't get hold of one and send it out of the park."

Charleston played eight seasons of winter ball in Cuba, where he also crushed Latino pitching. During those eight seasons, he compiled a .365 average, while winning batting titles in 1920 with .471, in 1922 with .446, and in 1924 with a .418 mark.

The 1923 Santa Clara club has been hailed as the greatest team in Cuban history, and it is often compared, like the 1935 Crawfords, to the 1927 New York Yankees. The outfield trio of Charleston, Alejandro Ohms, and Pablo Mesa compares well to any outfield ever assembled. Charleston hit .377 and established the Cuban record for stolen bases with 31. Sam Jethroe erased Charleston's standard 20 years later with 32.

Back in the United States, Charleston returned to his first club, the Indianapolis ABCs, for the 1922 and 1923 seasons. He hit .366 in 1922, but fell off to only .310 in 1923. He picked up the pace of his sub-par year in the fall when he joined the Detroit Stars for a three-game exhibition series against the St. Louis Browns. During the series, Turkey Stearnes hit third, Charleston fourth, and big John Beckwith fifth. These three stand among the most powerful hitters in black baseball history and presented the Browns with a murderers' row of extraordinary magnitude.

The Browns rolled to a 6–1 lead in the first game, but then the big bats began to boom. After Stearnes doubled in two runs, Charleston drove him in with a blistering single. Beckwith then tied the score with a long home run. In the ninth, Ed Wesley hit his second round tripper of the day and the Stars beat the Browns 7–6.

Detroit prevailed in the second game, again by the score of 7–6, as Oscar contributed three more hits. The Browns salvaged the final game 11–8, although Charleston had two hits including a homer.

In 1924, a savage baseball war began in black baseball as easterner Ed Bolden went after the best players in Rube Foster's NNL, among whom Charleston was the best. Charleston jumped from Indianapolis to the Harrisburg, Pennsylvania Giants where he once more anchored one of baseball's all-time best outfields. Teaming with the multi-talented Rap Dixon and fleet-footed Fats Jenkins, a member of the Basketball Hall of Fame, Charleston led the way by hitting .391 with eight homers in 54 games. He had still another big year in 1925, batting .418 and slamming 23 doubles along with 16 homers.

That fall, playing with the Lincoln Giants in an exhibition game in the Bronx, Charleston played against Columbia's Lou Gehrig. The Lincolns lost 6–5, but Charleston went four-for-six and made a spectacular catch in center field, besting Gehrig who went one-for-two.

Charleston slumped to .275 in 1926, but several post-season victories over Lefty Grove and the Philadelphia Athletics sweetened the season. The blacks took special pleasure in beating Grove, who voiced his racial prejudice loudly and often. Charleston preserved a 3–0 victory over Grove in Bloomsburg, Pennsylvania, with a great running catch in deepest center field. Another time, he slammed a homer off Grove in a 6–1 win.

In Bloomsburg, Grove, who even dared to drive Babe Ruth off the plate, knocked Charleston down. Ruth just laughed when Lefty knocked him down, but Charleston reacted quite differently. He stood up and fixed Grove with his smoldering eyes, dropped his bat, and then sprinted for the mound.

Grove, less than timid himself, came forward to meet Charleston, but at the last moment turned and ran away. Charleston stopped and yelled, "I knew you were yellow. Why don't you fight me like a man. I thought you weren't afraid of black guys?"

Grove responded by asking Jimmie Foxx to help him. "Hell, Lefty," said the amused Foxx, "I can't do that. He's my friend."

Once in a while, Charleston displayed a sense of humor, even about racial issues. In a Pittsburgh restaurant, the waitress told him, "We don't serve niggers here." "That's fine," replied Charleston, "I didn't plan to order one." He did receive service.

Charleston hit .335 for Harrisburg in 1927 and then joined Bolden's Philadelphia Hilldale club for 1928 and 1929, when he hit .335 and .360 respectively. In 1930, as financial pressures nearly destroyed black baseball, Charleston signed with Cum Posey's Homestead Grays, an independent barnstorming team. The aging Charleston ceased playing the outfield and danced a stylish first base for the Grays while hitting .333 in 1930 and .396 in 1931.

Then in 1932 the call came from Gus Greenlee and Charleston became the playing manager of the Crawfords. Now 36, Charleston hit only .271 for the season, and perhaps seeking some security, became somewhat of a company man for Greenlee. Cool Papa Bell recalls two incidents during his time with the Crawfords when his pride conflicted with Charleston's company attitude. "One time," Bell says, "they hired Babe Didrikson to pitch against us in a series of exhibition games. Charleston told us not to hit her because we needed her as a gate attraction. So the first time we went up against her, I bunted for a single. When I got back in the dugout, Charleston screamed at me, 'I thought I told you not to hit her.' I told him I didn't hit her, I just bunted. He said, 'Well, it's just the same. Don't do it again.' So I didn't bunt the next time; I hit a double off the wall. Charleston came running out of the dugout and I thought he was going to start swinging at me. Well, lucky for me, Josh Gibson came out and took my part. Charleston wasn't going to try anything with Josh there. But one thing's for sure, I wasn't going to let Charleston or anybody else tell me not to do my best on the baseball field.

"One other time, the Crawfords scheduled a donkey baseball game. Can you believe it, a donkey baseball game? I told Charleston I had pride and I wasn't going to make a fool out of myself by riding a donkey and trying to play baseball. He said he would fire me, but I knew Greenlee wouldn't let him do that. Anyway, I didn't play in that game."

Charleston hit .376 in 1933 and led the Crawfords to a second place finish during the first half of the NNL season, one game behind the Chicago American Giants. When the league failed to complete the second half of the schedule, the American Giants claimed the pennant, only to be overruled by Greenlee on behalf of his own club.

Charleston also proved during the 1933 season that he had lost none of his aggressiveness despite being 37 years old. "In one game in Pittsburgh between the Grays and Craws," says Buck Leonard, "Charleston put our catcher out for a month. His name was Fred Burnett. Everybody called him Tex. Poor guy. He tried to block the plate and Charleston just undressed him, cut off his uniform, his shin guards, everything."

Both Charleston and the Crawfords slumped in 1934. Oscar hit only .289 and the team dropped from a .714 winning percentage in 1933 to .630, which was still excellent, but fell short of making the pennant play-offs.

While Charleston hit just .288 in 1935, the Crawfords bounced back and made the play-offs against the New York Cubans. The Cubans, however, won the first two of a best-of-seven series. The Crawfords prevailed 3–0 in the third game as Gibson drove in one run with a triple, Bell did the same, and manager Charleston slammed the longest homer of the year in Dyckman's Oval.

The great Martin Dihigo, winner of the first game, put the Crawfords in a deep hole by winning the fourth. Pittsburgh won the fifth game, but found themselves trailing 6–3 in the ninth inning of the sixth contest. Charleston, still a great clutch hitter, blasted a three-run shot to tie the score. A few minutes later, Judy Johnson slapped a single to right field, driving home the winning run and forcing a seventh game.

Manager Martin Dihigo sent lefthander Luis Tiant, father of the future Red Sox star, to the mound for the deciding confrontation. The Cubans led 7–5 after seven innings, but in the eighth, Gibson and Charleston hit back-to-back homers to tie the score. Cool Papa Bell drove home Sammy Bankhead with the winning run and the Crawfords walked away with the championship in one of the greatest comebacks in baseball history.

Charleston's hitting heroics didn't surprise Jimmie Crutchfield. "Charleston used to complain that it wan't fun to hit anymore with the bases empty. As he got older, it became more and more important for him to hit in the clutch or with men on base. He just loved it. It didn't make any difference what his average was, how many hits he had in the game, or anything else. When it was clutch time, Charleston was still the toughest hitter in baseball."

The Crawfords won the second half of the 1936 split season, as the aging Charleston slipped to a .211 batting average. There were no play-offs, so the Crawfords traveled west for the annual national semi-pro Denver Post Tournament. The Craws dominated the competition and divided $5,000 in prize money, much needed in the hard Depression times.

The Crawfords then went on a barnstorming tour which included a stop in Mexico City, where they expected to play some Mexican teams. Instead, they met a team of major leaguers led by future Hall-of-Famers Jimmie Foxx, Heinie Manush, and Rogers Hornsby (who decided to play against blacks this time). Behind 4–2 in the ninth, the Crawfords rallied. Sammy Bankhead tripled and pinch-hitter "Spoony" Palm homered to tie the score. With two outs, Judy Johnson singled, Gibson walked, and the ever present Charleston singled to drive in Johnson with the lead run. Crutchfield then singled Gibson home and the Craws led 6–4.

Pittsburgh seemed to have the game iced with two outs in the bottom of the ninth, when Manush reached base on an error. Jimmie Foxx then slammed a 3–2 pitch over the fence to tie the score. The game continued scoreless into the bottom of the eleventh, when the All-Stars loaded the bases with one out. Foxx ripped a grounder toward the shortstop hole, but third baseman Johnson cut it off, wheeled back to his right, and forced the runner at the plate with a quick sidearm flip. Hornsby then forced Foxx at second to end the inning. As the Crawfords came in to hit in the top of the inning, the umpire suddenly called the game. "The sun's still in the sky," protested Bell, but much to the Crawfords' displeasure, the game ended in a 6–6 tie.

That evening, Charleston, Bell, and Foxx dined together in an expensive downtown Mexico City restaurant. Before they ate, Foxx indicated he would pick up the tab. "I think I owe you guys something," he said. "First of all, it was wrong to call the game with so much light left. Also, remember I hit the tying homer on a 3–2 pitch. Well, the pitch the umpire called ball three was really a strike. I shoulda' been outta' there."

Charleston's eyes smoldered and he snapped, "As usual, we Negroes get the short end of the deal. We do appreciate you though, Foxx. You're a friend and you always give us the credit we deserve as ball players."

The golden era of the Crawfords was over. The next spring, Rafael Trujillo's agents from the Dominican Republic began waving big money in front of Charleston's players. When Charleston caught one of the agents offering money, he grabbed the man by the throat and told him to give his money to the whites. His efforts proved futile, however, as Satchel, Josh, Cool Papa, Sammy Bankhead, Leroy Matlock, and Bill Perkins all left the Crawfords to play for Trujillo.

Charleston went to bat just 10 times in 1937 with only one hit to show for his efforts. The Crawfords wallowed near the bottom of the pack, playing less than .500 ball for a season for the first time in the team's history.

Charleston left Pittsburgh to manage the Toledo Crawfords and then the Philadelphia Stars. He also managed the Brooklyn Brown Bombers, a team which played on Ebbets Field and was used as a front by Branch Rickey to scout Jackie Robinson, Roy Campanella, and other talented black prospects. Charleston urged Rickey to sign Campanella, who went on to become the second black man elected to the Hall of Fame. Robinson, of course, was the first.

At the end of his career, Charleston went back home to manage the Indianapolis Clowns, a ridiculous version of the great black teams of yesteryear. The Clowns once featured first baseman "Goose" Tatum of Harlem Globetrotter basketball fame and served as a major league stepping stone for a young right-handed slugger named Henry Aaron.

How tragic for Oscar Charleston to finish his career managing a team which clowned more than they played serious baseball. Perhaps the greatest of them all, Oscar Charleston never escaped from the shadows.

$$\frac{8}{\text{Mr. Sunshine}}$$

If Johnson were only white, he could write his own

price.

Connie Mack, Hall of Fame Manager
Philadelphia Athletics

*W*illiam Johnson, known to almost everyone as Judy, except Josh Gibson who called him "Jing," commanded enormous respect among his peers. They remember his great baseball intelligence, his clutch hitting, and his defensive brilliance at third base. Most of all, they remember him as a man of integrity.

Ted Page remembered once when Judy went to an extreme to do the right thing. "The Crawfords were playing in a small town somewhere, I don't remember where. Anyway, we arrived in this town fairly early in the morning and had a game that night. We found a place to stay, but the place was little more than a collection of shacks about a mile from town. Well, Judy decided he needed a haircut. Some of the boys cut their own hair, but not Judy, he wanted a regular barber. Now, they weren't going to drive the bus just to get one man into town, so Judy walked the mile to get his haircut. For some reason, he didn't take quite enough money with him. He was one penny short of having enough to pay the barber. The guy told him to forget it, but not Judy. He walked back to where we were staying, got the penny, and walked back into town to give it to the barber. Of course, a penny meant more then than it does now, but not many guys would walk two miles to give a man a penny. The barber was at the game that night, and he made a big issue of pointing Judy out and telling everybody that he was the most honest man he'd ever seen."

"Judy was the best," says Cool Papa Bell. "You could trust him in every way. I would trust him with my life and with my money. He would never let you down. He was always up and optimistic. He brought sunshine into your life. Judy Johnson and Jimmie Crutchfield are the two finest people I met in baseball."

Crutchfield says "Judy was a steadying influence on the Crawfords. He had a great mind. He anticipated plays and always seemed to know what the opponents were going to do. And nobody stole more signs."

According to the Crawfords' little left-handed spitballer, Sam Streeter, "I knew hitters pretty well. The Crawfords had several good clutch hitters. Everybody talked about Charleston as a clutch hitter. Josh was a good clutch hitter and so were Bell and Crutchfield. But Judy was the best of them all. When you had men on base, Judy was the guy you wanted up there."

"You talk about playing third base," said Ted Page. "Judy was better than anybody I ever saw, and I saw Pie Traynor, Brooks Robinson, and Mike Schmidt. He had a powerful accurate arm. He could do everything, come in for a ball, cut it off at the line, or range way over toward the shortstop hole. He was really something."

Judy Johnson, Mr. Sunshine

William Julius Johnson, the future baseball genius, was born in Snow Hill, Maryland, on October 26, 1899, the second of three children. His father, a seaman, moved the family from Snow Hill to Wilmington, Delaware, in the early 1900s. When Billy, as he was known as a boy, turned 8, his father began grooming him as a prizefighter. The elder Johnson bought two pairs of boxing gloves, one for young Billy and another for his 12-year-old sister, Mary Emma, who was quite a tomboy.

"My father had Emma and me box," Judy remembered. "But it just wasn't fair. She was pretty tough to begin with and I couldn't hit her in the face, the chest, or the stomach. So where was I supposed to hit her? I took some pretty good lickings. I decided pretty quick that I didn't want to be a boxer.

"I was much more interested in playing baseball. I went right out my back door into a park and that's where I started playing baseball. It was more of a pasture than anything else, with cows and horses in there grazing. After school, we'd clean it off and play until dark.

"My father was the athletic director of the Negro Settlement House in our neighborhood and so I always had bats and balls. I think that's the only reason the other kids let me play, because I really wasn't very good at that time.

"My father had a baseball team called the Royal Blues and he gave me his glove. I could hardly keep it on my hand because of the rot. I kept it until it completely fell apart. He finally bought me a new glove, but compared to what they use now, it looked like a dress glove or something you'd use to keep your hands warm.

"For my first baseball shoes, I bought spikes and had a shoemaker put them on a regular pair of shoes. I thought I was going to be a real big-timer then. But I made a big mistake, and I looked pretty silly. I forgot to have him take the heels off and I had to walk and run kind of tipped forward."

As a teenager, Johnson began playing for Wilmington's Rosedale club which played both black and white teams in the area. "We used to walk miles to play," Judy remembered. "We were pretty dedicated to the game. We usually drew a good crowd and we'd pass the hat to get enough money to buy balls for the next game."

After almost every game, Judy tried to spend time at the home of Rosedale's team captain so he could get to know the boy's sister Anita. "We got to know each other pretty well," Judy said. "She'd walk me to the corner and I'd give her a hit-and-run kiss and be on my way."

Judy and Anita became so well-acquainted that they married in 1924, their union lasting until her death in 1986. "Anita was the most precious part of my life," Judy said, "even baseball was second to her."

Disappointed in Howard High School because of its lack of a sports program, Judy left school after his freshman year and obtained a job as a stevedore in Deep Water Point, New Jersey. He worked there through World War I and then returned home and began playing for the Chester Giants in Pennsylvania for $5 a game and transportation. In 1918, he signed with the Philadelphia Hilldale team and was placed on the roster of the Madison Stars, a farm club for the big team. Still, he earned miniscule wages.

During his time with Madison, Johnson played with a veteran outfielder named Robert "Judy" Gans, whom he strongly resembled. He thus acquired the nickname that would remain with him for the rest of his life.

Hilldale's owner, Ed Bolden, purchased Johnson's contract from Madison in 1920 for $100 and the youngster became an understudy to veteran third baseman Bill "Brodie" Francis. "Francis was very good to me," Judy said. "He taught me a lot about playing third base even though he knew I was eventually going to take his job.

"As a young player, they tried to test me out by bunting, and at first they were very successful. I didn't handle the bunts very well. But Francis worked on it with me for hours and hours. I was trying to field a bunt, stand up, and then throw. Of course, that didn't work very well. Francis taught me to come in, grab the ball with my bare hand, and throw all in one motion. He taught me to throw underhand or across my body as the situation called for. I sure surprised some of those boys and they stopped trying to bunt on me."

"Another guy I like on that team was Bill Pettus. He played first base and he'd take all the stuffing out of his mitt and put in chicken feathers. Every time he caught the ball, chicken feathers would go flying. I can still see it.

"Now, Louis Santop was a little tougher to get along with. He was a big star and one of the best hitters I ever saw. He could hit the ball a mile. But he knew he was a star and I was just a little guy. So I wound up carrying his equipment around for most the season."

The following year in 1921, Judy became the regular third baseman for Hilldale. Despite carrying only 150 pounds on his 5'11" frame, Johnson established a reputation for toughness and durability. "I didn't know Judy in those days," says Cool Papa Bell, "but he was gaining a reputation as being tough, a good clutch hitter, a great defensive player and, above all, a gentleman. When I got to know him, playing both against him and with him, I knew it was all true."

"I was never a great hitter," Judy said, "but I always figured a way to get on base. I threw from the right side and I hit from the right side, so I would have the left sleeve just a little baggier than the right. I'd just lean in and let the ball tick my sleeve or I'd puff my shirt out in the front and let the ball tick me there. Minnie Minoso was another guy who was good at getting hit when he needed to get on base."

Judy earned $150 a month during the season playing for Hilldale. It was big money for him, but considerably less than the players in Rube Foster's NNL, who averaged nearly $300 a month. He bought a new glove, which was a practice he continued each year for the rest of his career. "I'd break in the new glove and then save it just for games. I used the old glove for practice. I also carried two pairs shoes, one for good fields and one for bad ones. You just wouldn't believe how much junk there was on some of the fields we played on."

During the 1921 season, even though Judy was just a rookie, some began to compare him with the legendary Creole third baseman, Oliver "The Ghost" Marcelle of New Orleans. The dashing Marcelle played third base with skill and intelligence seldom seen. He feared nothing and nobody, once even daring to start a fight with Oscar Charleston. Many believed Johnson played third with equal skill and intelligence, and despite the young man's quiet nature, he proved he could not be intimidated by psychological pressure, knockdown pitches, or flashing spikes.

In later years, Johnson acknowledged that being compared to Marcelle was a great honor. "I could outhit him," Judy said, "and I could run faster. But he made all the plays look so easy. I'll tell you this, I played five winter seasons in Cuba with Marcelle. Guess who played third base? It wasn't me. I played second."

Following the 1921 season, Rube Foster came East with his American Giants to play the Atlantic City Bacharach Giants and Hilldale to determine the best black team in America. The American Giants beat the Bacharachs two games to one.

Hilldale met the American Giants at Philadelphia's Shibe Park and lost the first game, 5–2, but then reeled off three consecutive wins. Judy keyed the third game victory with a triple and a homer.

When Ed Bolden formed the Eastern Colored League in 1923, he assured the dominance of his own Hilldale club by signing some of the best players in black baseball, including John Henry Lloyd. Johnson remembers Lloyd well. "Mr. Connie Mack believed Honus Wagner and John Lloyd were the two greatest shortstops of all time. John taught me more baseball than anyone else. He showed me how to protect myself. We had more trouble with violence among our black boys than we did with whites. They always used to talk about Ty Cobb sharpening his spikes, well, it seemed like all our boys sharpened their spikes with files. My legs used to get all cut up. I learned about wearing shin guards from Lloyd.

Judy Johnson

He also taught to watch runners coming into base and to decide if they were gonna come straight in or use a hook slide. He showed me how to decoy guys by pretending as if the ball wasn't coming and then making the tag at the very last second.

"Despite all of John's help I had a bad experience the one time mother came to see me play. She never really wanted to come to a game, but I finally got her there one Sunday in Philly. A runner was trying to steal third and, as usual, I put my foot down to block the base. This guy came up high when I tried to tag him and tore my face open. Mother fainted in the stands and never came to see me play again. But it only took five stitches to sew me up."

While Hilldale won the 1923 Eastern League pennant, Rube Foster, still angry because of the player raids on his NNL, refused to play a World Series. The following season, with Judy's .327 average leading the way, Hilldale again won the Eastern championship. This time, Foster approved of a World Series between Hilldale and the Kansas City Monarchs, the first modern championship in black baseball history. Despite a sparkling performance by Johnson, including a game-winning inside-the-park homer, Kansas City won the series five games to four. Hilldale avenged their defeat in the 1925 World Series, devastating the Monarchs five games to one, as Johnson hit an even .300.

During the winter, Judy joined many black stars in Palm Beach, Florida, where two rival hotels, the Breakers and the Poinciana, hired them to provide baseball entertainment for the guests. The hotels paid the men well, but the real lure was the big money to be won in floating crap games or by running rum from nearby Cuba to prohibition United States.

Johnson just played baseball, skipping the gambling and rum. Still, he remembered the winter in Palm Beach well. "They used to stack the boxes and cases of rum right up to the ceiling of the room I stayed in. Sure was plenty of money being made.

"One night, a couple of white men broke into my room, shined a flashlight in my face, and asked where my brother was. I guess they meant George Johnson, the outfielder, who was no relation. I told them I didn't know where he was and they left me alone. I suppose he owed them some money or something. Anyway, it was a close call.

"One of the other guys was not so lucky. His name was "Rube" Chambers, a good left-hander for the Lincoln Giants. They found him shot to death in a railroad boxcar. He must have crossed the wrong guy."

Although Judy hit .302, Oliver Marcelle and the Bacharach Giants won the Eastern League crown in 1926. Instead of playing in the Black World Series then, Hilldale played a four-game exhibition series against a team of white major leaguers led by Heinie Manush and Jimmy Dykes. Hilldale won three of four and earned more money per man than had they played in the Series.

"It was good to win," Judy said, "and I appreciated the money, but the best was beating Lefty Grove. He just hated us. It was nigger this and nigger that. I never wanted a hit so bad in my life as the first time I came up against him. I hit the first pitch he threw me right back at him. It took the cap right off his head and went into center field for a single. Grove was pretty rattled. He didn't say anything for quite a while. Me? I couldn't have been happier. I remember that hit more than any I ever got."

While Judy hit .372 in Cuba during the 1927 winter season and .329 the next season, his average for Hilldale fell below .300 both seasons. He bounced back to hit a resounding .416 in 1929.

The Eastern Colored League folded in 1930, and Johnson jumped to the independent Homestead Grays. He returned to Hilldale in 1931 and remained there until early 1932 when he joined Greenlee and the Crawfords.

Judy remembered Gus Greenlee well. "He certainly was a high roller. He carried loads of $100 bills in his pockets and he'd always give you a few bucks if you needed it. He once paid me a nice piece of change to chauffeur him to Chicago.

"I don't think Gus had any idea just how much money he had. He probably would have gone broke sooner than he did if his wife hadn't saved some of his money.

"Gus was a gangster, you know, and everybody knew he carried all that money. I know it sounds strange, but he never had any bodyguards. Everybody was afraid to fool with Gus. Not only did he have power, but he was a tough man. They say Al Capone killed some people with his bare hands. Well, I don't think Gus ever killed anybody, but he could have done it with his bare hands too. He was a very big, very tough man.

"Gus and Charley didn't have us practice on our days off, which were rare, because they knew we needed the rest. So when we did get a day off, we would go to a big league game to see if we could learn anything. They let us in free in every park except St. Louis. There we had to pay and then sit in a section just for colored people.

"I enjoyed going to Pirates games more than any other because I liked to watch their third baseman Pie Traynor, who was probably the best in the game at that time. Crutch also liked the Pirates because he was a big fan of the Waner Brothers.

"Now, Josh Gibson just loved Yankee Stadium. He loved to see Ruth and Gehrig hit any time he could. Cool liked to see the Athletics because he was a big fan of Jimmy Foxx. Strange, Cool and Foxx were very different kinds of players, but Cool really liked to see him play."

Johnson made a major contribution to the Crawfords during their glory years. While his batting averages from 1932–1936 read only .246, .239, .243, .257, and .235, he remained, like Oscar Charleston, a great clutch hitter and an excellent defensive player. Judy retired after the 1936 season when Greenlee wanted to sell him back to the Homestead Grays. Although angered by Greenlee's deal, he had fond memories of his days with the Crawfords.

"I played on some great teams," he said. "Those Hilldale clubs and the Homestead Grays were exceptional. But the Crawfords were the best. First of all, we had great team spirit. Everybody got along real well. No jealousy. We had some big stars, Satch, Josh, Cool, Charley, but none of them was the jealous type at all.

They wanted the team to win and they didn't worry about who picked up the pitching victory or who got the game-winning hit. They wanted everybody to do well.

"Everybody knows the Crawfords had great hitting and they know we had Satchel. We had other pretty good pitchers too. No better spitballer than little Sam Streeter. Leroy Matlock was a top left-hander. Harry Kincannon. Bertrum Hunter, everybody called him Nat. Theolic Smith, we called him 'Fireball.' All those guys were tough pitchers. We had more than just Satchel.

"Don't forget our defense either. It was great. I was past my prime when I played for the Crawfords, and so was Charleston. But we used our heads and we could both still do it defensively.

"Our outfield of Bell, Crutchfield, and Page was outstanding, and got even better when Sammy Bankhead played with Cool and Crutch. Bankhead was a wonderful outfielder with one of the greatest arms of all time. And how could you find a greater defensive outfielder than Cool. Crutchfield? Well, he could do it all, a very underrated player.

"Our double play combination was also one of the best. At shortstop we had Chester Williams who made the East-West game almost every year. When Bankhead played short we lost nothing. At second, we had John Henry Russell, 'Pistol Johnny,' a fine player. Later, we had Dick Seay, and as Jimmie Crutchfield used to say, 'Seay could turn a double play with a frog.' "

The Crawfords held the same high opinion of Johnson. Cool Papa Bell says, "Judy was a great man to be around. Things often got tough for us, and when they did, Judy would always say, 'Just keep goin' boys, the Sun will be shining up there ahead someplace.' "

9

The Black Mafia

Most of our baseball was run by gangsters. They were slick and smooth. Sometimes dangerous. I didn't trust very many of them.

Clint Thomas, Outfielder
New York Black Yankees

During the 1920s, with Prohibition in full swing, most of important white gangsters considered the numbers game beneath their dignity. Numbers operations, therefore, became the stronghold of black organized crime. During this time, Alessandro Pompez, owner of the Cuban Stars, and later the New York Cubans, established himself as the Harlem numbers king.

Born of Cuban parents in Key West, Florida, Pompez became a baseball manager and sports promoter even as a young man. He was, in fact, one of the men who negotiated the agreement that created the first Black World Series in 1924.

Pompez gained prominence in Harlem by becoming a protégé of the notorious Jewish gangster, Arthur Flegenheimer, better known as Dutch Schultz, the Beer Baron of the Bronx. Schultz's territory extended well into Manhattan and Pompez secured his initial bankrolling from him. Pompez continued his association with Schultz, but also maintained his independence. By 1930 he was one of Harlem's best known celebrities and wealthiest men, and owner of Dyckman's Oval, the amusement and baseball park.

As Prohibition ended, Schultz began searching for new areas of profit. He and the financial wizard of his operation, Otto "Abbadabba" Berman, focused on the numbers racket and began moving in on Pompez and others. Rather than face the guns of Schultz's enforcers, Abe Landau and Bernard "Lulu" Rosenkrantz, Pompez became an employee of the organization. Schultz continued to provide political, physical, and financial protection and Pompez continued to prosper, although less than before.

Meanwhile, the Internal Revenue Service began to pursue Schultz, and on November 29, 1934, the front page of the *New York Times* reported: "Dutch Schultz Surrenders." Because of the Dutchman's New York City notoriety, his lawyers succeeded in obtaining a change of venue for his tax evasion trial, first to Syracuse, New York, and then to the small upstate community of Malone, New York.

Schultz went to Malone well before the trial, living in the town and working to establish rapport with the community people. He visited the local hospital with flowers and candy for the patients. He threw a lavish grand ball to which everyone in town was invited. By the time of the trial, the people of Malone viewed Schultz as a good man who was being picked on by the Feds. Predictably, a mistrial in the form of a "hung jury" resulted.

In 1935 Democratic Governor Herbert Lehman of New York appointed Republican Thomas Dewey, a former United States attorney, as a special prosecutor. Dewey went right after Schultz, threatening to convene a grand jury to investigate The Dutchman's activities. As the pressure increased Schultz became even more unpredictable, murdering one of his top men, Bo Weinberg, and even threatening to kill Dewey. Lucky Luciano, head of New York's most powerful family, along with many other leading gangsters, rejected the idea of assassinating Dewey because of the heat that would ensue.

In addition to being upset with Schultz because of the Dewey situation, Luciano also wanted to take over The Dutchman's lucrative operations. The two factors spelled doom for Schultz. On the evening of October 25, 1935, Schultz dined with Berman, Landau, and Rosenkrantz at the Palace Steak and Chop House in Newark, New Jersey, the unofficial headquarters of his organization. Schultz left the group to visit the men's room and two professional gunmen, Charles "Charlie the Bug" Workman, and Emmanuel "Mendy" Weiss, entered the establishment and blasted the henchman with shotguns. They also went to the men's room and shot Schultz, who died less than a day later.

With Schultz gone, Alex Pompez regained his lost power. Dewey, however, needing an adversary to fuel his lofty political ambitions, turned his attention to Pompez. He spent sixteen months preparing a master plan to destroy Pompez and his Harlem rackets.

Just by coincidence, Dewey put his plan into motion early in 1937 as he prepared to run for the New York governorship. One day, as Pompez returned to his office just off Lenox Avenue, he sensed something was amiss as soon as he entered the elevator. The elevator operator, friendly to Pompez, kept bobbing his head up and down while raising his eyebrows. Pompez and his assistant, Cuban pitcher Juan Mirabel, stepped off the elevator several floors below the office, climbed down a nearby fire escape, and disappeared into the masses of Harlem. Instead of nabbing Pompez, Dewey's men had to be satisfied with the confiscation of $34,000 in cash.

Assisted by a network of friends, Pompez eluded the Feds and crossed into Mexico near Tucson, Arizona. In Mexico, Pompez continued his flashy life-style, and pressured by Dewey, the Mexican federales arrested him as he stepped into a bulletproof limousine bearing Illinois license plates. Pompez's influence extended to the upper reaches of the Mexican government, however, and Dewey's request for extradition was declined.

Pompez still longed to return home and did so when promised immunity from prosecution if he turned state's evidence against the mob. The usual reward for such activities was a swim with the fishes, as gangland assassinations were often called, but somehow, Pompez managed to escape retribution.

Leaving behind his gangster days, Pompez focused his considerable energies on baseball, building the New York Cubans into a powerful NNL pennant contender during the 1940s. He used the Polo grounds as a home field and became a close friend of New York Giants' owner Horace Stoneham. Using his connections, Pompez acted as an agent in the signings of many Latin American players, including Puerto Rican Orlando Cepeda, son of his old friend Perucho.

In 1948, Pompez concluded a deal with his friend Stoneham to make the Cubans a New York Giant farm club, thereby becoming the only Negro League team ever having a formal agreement with a major league organization. The former gangster rose to be one of the most respected baseball men in America and sat as an original member of the Hall of Fame's Negro League Committee which selected the first of the old-time black stars for induction.

Gus Greenlee traveled to Harlem a number of times during the middle 1920s to see Pompez and learn how to run the numbers game. The two became close friends and Pompez bankrolled Greenlee's successful effort to gain control of black Pittsburgh's numbers racket.

While never as respected as Pompez, Greenlee was nevertheless well liked by most of his players. "He took care of us," Ted Page said. "One winter, I had no job and my wife didn't want to go South for winter ball because her mother was living with us and she was sick. I didn't want to go without Juanita, so I didn't know what I was going to do.

"Well, along comes Gus to offer me quite a job. I was a numbers lookout. Now Gus had the cops and most everybody paid off, but there were a few who wouldn't take his money and some others who were jealous of him or wanted to take over his business. So, it was important for him not to get caught with numbers money.

"All I had to do was sit in a chair by the side door of the Crawford Grille from 11 o'clock in the morning until 3 o'clock in the afternoon six days a week. The Grille was a big, sprawling two-story place. The bottom floor was a restaurant and a cabaret. Upstairs, they had a few prostitutes, but most of it was devoted to running the numbers business.

"While Gus and his men counted the day's money upstairs, I just sat outside and watched. I was supposed to ring a bell if anybody suspicious came around. I never had to ring the bell once and Gus paid me $15 a month all winter long. That was pretty good money for Depression times."

Cool Papa Bell once feared for the life of a youngster who snitched on the numbers operation. "There was a young boy who worked around the numbers rooms cleaning up," Bell says. "One time, he tipped off a couple of the cops who wanted to get Gus. He told them the time most of the numbers money would be delivered. They pulled a raid and Greenlee lost plenty. I heard talk about killing the boy, so I went to Greenlee and begged him to let the boy go. I even offered to pay for a train ticket to send him to another town. I don't think Gus even knew about the kid. All he said was, 'I'm not going to have any boy killed.' "

"All I know is that as soon as I told Greenlee, the boy was safe and on his way out of town on a train. They didn't use my money."

"Gus Greenlee was no killer," said Judy Johnson. "One time, though, I did hear a rumor about him having some guys bumped off. They were a couple of black guys who tried to get money from people for protection. You know how it goes, pay me and nothing will happen to you. But if you don't pay me, something will happen for sure.

"Well, these guys started taking money from little people like pool hall owners, and grocery store owners. Gus sincerely cared about the community and he didn't like the protection stuff at all. I guess he saw himself as the community's protection. Anyway, those guys weren't around too long and I heard they were at the bottom of the river.

"As I said, I think Gus really cared about the community. He stayed away from stuff that really hurt people, stuff like protection, dope, and loan sharking.

"Gus did have a few prostitutes upstairs at the Grille. They were pretty expensive too. I heard it was $50 for a full night if business was slow, and $100 for the night if business was going good.

"I know Gus could get rough if he had to. I guess during Prohibition he used to hijack liquor trucks coming down from Canada. Now, some of that stuff belonged to people like Lucky Luciano and Dutch Schultz. So Gus wasn't afraid to mess around with the big boys."

Some of the other black gangsters were far less community-minded than Greenlee according to Willie Wells. "Some of those guys would do anything including killing people. The first guy I played for was Dick Kent with the St. Louis Stars and he certainly had very little conscience about anything. He was into protection, drugs, loan-sharking, all kinds of bad stuff."

"When I was with the New York Black Yankees," said Ted Page, the owner was Ed Semler. They called him 'Soldier Boy.' He was crazy. He was so bad that Lucky Luciano told him to go to Chicago with the other crazy people. Luciano wasn't happy with all the gangster killings and thought the streets of Chicago weren't safe for anybody. He thought Semler would fit in well there.

"Another bad guy was Robert Cole," said Wells. "He had taken over Rube Foster's team in Chicago and called them Cole's American Giants. I went there in 1932, but things were real bad financially. The team was going bankrupt and Cole came to me and told me he'd put my salary in a special account if I'd convince the other players to go without salaries in hopes of a better day. I told him where to go real quick."

Rufus "Sonnyman" Jackson, the Homestead
Grays' Gangster Connection.

When Gus Greenlee decided to renew the NNL, he realized that black baseball faced the same problem as Robert Cole, lack of money. He turned to the only source of financing he knew, the other black gangsters. Their money breathed continuing life into black baseball.

Baseball, of course, also proved advantageous to the gangster/owners. They could launder the money gained from illegal activities in the guise of baseball revenue and thus avoid paying large amounts of income tax. White society's ignorance of black baseball helped the gangsters carry off the deception, as did the fact that both baseball admissions and gambling receipts were usually cash.

Gangster money offered black baseball its only chance of survival during the Great Depression and even the highly respected Cum Posey recognized the fact. Posey, a legitimate businessman, whose only discernable vice was occasional gambling, turned to the notorious gangster Rufus "Sonnyman" Jackson to provide financial support to keep his Homestead Grays afloat during the hard times of the 1930s. Like the other shadow operators, Jackson welcomed the opportunity as a way to hide some of his underground activities.

Jackson had migrated north to Pittsburgh from Columbus, Georgia, and secured a job in the steel mills. Before long, however, he began earning his living as the promoter of various enterprises. He became owner of a large tavern called The Skyrocket, which included a restaurant, and he also invested in several lucrative gambling houses where people could indulge almost any gaming urge, be it craps, poker, blackjack, or any one of a variety of other games. The "Sonnyman" also became king of the "piccolos," nickelodeons and jukeboxes, running as many as 500 up and down the Allegheny and Monongahela Rivers.

Jackson often resorted to violence and various strong-arm measures to achieve his ends, but in April of 1935, he nearly tasted some of his own medicine. Four extortionists demanded $500 from Jackson on threat of death. They wanted the cash to be left at an abandoned shack near the Homestead Bridge at 2 o'clock in the morning.

Just before 2 o'clock, Jackson drove up and deposited the money as directed. He had called the FBI, however, and inside the shack waited twenty-five well-armed agents. Jackson ran for his life as a gunfight broke out between the feds and the extortionists, who managed to escape.

Cum Posey, despite his connection with the unscrupulous Jackson, stands as one of the shining lights of black baseball. His Homestead Grays remain one of the great dynasties in sports history, fielding powerhouse teams in the 1920s, the early 1930s, and from 1937–1945, winning nine straight NNL pennants.

Perhaps even more important, Posey ran a class organization and treated his players with dignity and respect. While sometimes in serious financial trouble, he always paid his men, a claim which can be made for very few owners of black teams. Posey also tried to provide the best possible working conditions for his players, paying careful attention to travel, lodging, food, equipment, and even emotional and social welfare.

Abe and Effa Manley, co-owners of the Newark Eagles, were also well liked and respected. They spent substantial sums of money on the team, much of it garnered from the numbers business, and while the Eagles proved to be a financial loss, Abe expressed satisfaction with the investment. "I got plenty," he said, "I saw boys I developed enter major league baseball. I saw Doby, Newcombe, and Irvin become stars."

Effa Manley

Effa Manley reigned as the glamour girl of black baseball. She met Abe at the 1932 World Series and they married soon after. The newlyweds loved baseball, and in 1935, they established a Negro National League franchise in Newark. Abe scouted and handled player development while Effa, who had brains in addition to her great beauty, conducted the team's business affairs. Once in awhile she interfered with the running of the club on the field, and this stands as the lone complaint against her by the team's managers and players.

Effa served as treasurer of the New Jersey NAACP, lending a strong voice for integration. She was also a charter member of the Citizens League for Fair Play. When this group desegregated Harlem department store employment in the 1930s, she stood at the forefront of the picket lines.

Cumberland Willis Posey, Founder of the
Homestead Grays.

Always outspoken, Effa erupted in 1948 when Jackie Robinson blasted black baseball and the difficult conditions for its players. "No greater ingratitude was ever displayed," she snorted.

She also took strong exception to Branch Rickey's comment that "The Negro League has the semblance of a racket."

"Who was he to criticize," she said. "Who was he to discuss illegal activities. He took players from the Negro League and didn't even pay for them. How legal is that. I'd call that a racket.

"Rickey tried to sign Monte Irvin without paying us a cent. When our lawyer got involved, Rickey just turned Irvin loose."

J. L. Wilkinson, a white man, and owner of the legendary Kansas City Monarchs, also commanded respect. Like the Manleys, he had been burned by Branch Rickey, who signed Jackie Robinson and paid the Monarchs nothing.

Wilkinson, along with Cum Posey, formed the strong unifying thread that kept black baseball alive from the time of Rube Foster's illness until major league integration. He also resembled Posey in his genuine concern for the welfare of his players. He traveled with his team, ate with them, and stayed with them at segregated hotels. As a white man, he could have stayed at the hotel of his choice, but instead, he remained with his team. Sometimes, the Monarchs solved the prejudice problem by camping out, often sharing meals with Depression pilgrims.

Wilkinson also initiated night baseball. It happened in Enid, Oklahoma, on April 28, 1930, when the Monarchs played a game against Phillips University. Wilkinson had been working on the idea for some time, developing a very effective system that featured individual telescoped steel poles which supported six 1000-watt lights on each pole. A Ford truck carried each of the poles, and they were positioned behind first, behind third, and across the outfield. The lights were fairly effective, and the Monarchs defeated Phillips 12–3 as baseball moved into the future.

The Black Mafia, in which Posey and Wilkinson are included only because they owned black teams, was comprised of men and women who represented the full spectrum of human nature. Some were saints, and some were sinners, while most, including Gus Greenlee, stood somewhere in between.

10
The Brotherhood

Because of baseball, I smelled the rose of life. I wanted to meet interesting people, to travel, and to have nice clothes. Baseball allowed me to do all those things, and most important, during my time with the Crawfords, it allowed me to become a member of a brotherhood of friendship which will last forever.

Cool Papa Bell, 1988
St. Louis, Missouri

*M*uch has been said about the good aspects of black baseball, and there were many. Much has also been said about the hardships, and there were many, especially the long bus trips, the endless games, the sleazy hotels, the poor food, and the dark encounters with racism. Through it all, the good times and the bad, a brotherhood of friendship sustained the men of the Crawfords.

Low salaries have been stressed as one of the most negative features of life in black baseball. When compared to the salaries of their major league contemporaries, the pay for blacks was indeed low, and a comparison with modern major league salaries becomes ridiculous. When compared to the earnings of most other black men, however, as well as most white men during the Depression, the compensation looms rather large.

This elevated financial status, combined with the power and glamour of being an athlete, put great pressure on the players to become role models for the black community. Suffering from segregation, and during the Crawfords' era, further impoverished by the Depression, America's black communities needed successful black men and women to emulate. Furthermore, the black players represented their team, their community, and their race. These responsibilities weighed heavy for such young men, especially since many of them originated from very unsophisticated backgrounds.

Meeting the responsibilities became an integral part of the professionalism in which the Crawfords took so much pride. Most did their best to lead highly moral lives, display good manners, dress well, and above all, be accessible to the fans.

According to Judy Johnson, Cool Papa Bell presented the perfect example for other black players and other black men. "When Cool and I played together in Pittsburgh, he was the most popular player on the team both among his teammates and the fans. All you had to do was walk down the street with him and you knew why. He was a beautiful dresser. Absolutely immaculate. He had perfect manners and you never heard him say even a 'hell' or a 'damm.'

"He had time for everybody. Never hurried. Signed autographs, talked to people, gave advice on baseball, anything they wanted. All the time showin' his big beautiful smile. He was so kind. If everybody was like Cool this would be a better world."

The 1935 Pittsburgh Crawfords in Spring
Training at Hot Springs, Arkansas.
Standing L-R, Jelly Taylor, Judy Johnson,
Leroy Matlock, unknown rookie, Josh Gibson,
Hood Witton, trainer
Middle, Cool Papa Bell, Sam Bankhead, Oscar
Charleston, Clarence Palm, Jimmie
Crutchfield, Spoon Carter, Bill Perkins
Seated, T. Bond, Howard, Nat Hunter, Sam
Streeter, Harry Kincannon, Duro Davis

While Bell, Judy Johnson, and Jimmie Crutchfield personified the classiest of black players, some of their contemporaries looked to the musicians for guidance and for friendship. The ball players viewed themselves essentially as entertainers and strongly identified with the life-styles of the musicians. They further identified with the music itself, with blues, jazz, and swing being unique extensions of their own cultural heritage.

Among the entertainers, Bill "Mr. Bojangles" Robinson was closest to black baseball and most of the players idolized him. Robinson's dancing wizardry stemmed from his great athletic ability. Once, having trained himself to run backward very quickly, he defeated future U.S. Congressman Ralph Metcalfe in a race, running backward 75 yards to Metcalfe's 100 yards forwards. While defeating a

The Mills Brothers

Congressman may seem less than impressive, it must be remembered that Metcalfe was a world-class sprinter who finished second to Jesse Owens in the 100 meters at the 1936 Berlin Olympic Games.

Robinson and Satchel Paige were close friends, and besides serving as the best man at The Master's wedding, Mr. Bojangles provided Paige with an insider's view of Harlem's sensuous nightlife. Whenever the Crawfords played in New York, the two high rollers made the rounds of the Cotton Club, Connie's Inn, and Small's Paradise, all at Robinson's expense.

When Robinson became owner of the New York Black Yankees in the late 1930s, he tried to infuse the team with class by purchasing old New York Yankee uniforms. Several of his players took great pride in wearing pinstripes which once belonged to superstars such as Lefty Gomez, Lou Gehrig, and Joe DiMaggio.

As Mr. Bojangles lay dying in a New York City hospital in 1949, he summoned Jackie Robinson and Roy Campanella to his deathbed. Holding each of their hands, he offered a tearful prayer for their continued success in the major leagues.

Louis Armstrong

Satchel Paige, the most visible of the Crawfords, became a favorite of the Mills Brothers, who called him "The Minstral of the Mound." Satchel also enjoyed the brothers and their music. When they played at the Crawford Grille, he often joined them in impromptu after-hours singing sessions. His fine voice and skillful guitar playing blended well with their famous mellow tones.

The brothers also loved baseball. They had their own Crawford uniforms made and sometimes traveled with the team. They enjoyed working out with the club before games. "They weren't great," recalled Judy Johnson, "but they didn't make fools out of themselves either."

Cool Papa Bell has a special fondness for Louis Armstrong. A knowledgeable baseball man, Armstrong sponsored a team in his hometown of New Orleans for several years. It was called Louis Armstrong's Secret Nine and featured some of the best black ball players in the city.

"Armstrong was just a wonderful man," Cool says. "He was a regular guy with no big head. He loved to talk baseball and he knew the game well. I spent time with him in Pittsburgh and in New York City. I guess he used to take some of the boys up to his house in Queens for some nice parties, but I didn't get in on any of those.

"I spent more time with him in California than back East. During the winter season, he used to come in the steam baths and sit there for hours discussing baseball. He never talked about music, just baseball. He was quite a man.

"I also liked Lena Horne very much and I got to know her pretty well. She was a beautiful lady, just striking. And she could sing and dance too. Her daddy, Teddy, was real proud of her."

The legendary Cab Calloway also sponsored a baseball team. Appropriate, if not original, he called the team Cab Calloway's All-Stars. He even played for the team.

"Cab Calloway stayed off by himself," says Jimmie Crutchfield. "My favorite was Duke Ellington."

For Ted Page, piano genius Fats Waller was the man. "Every time we played in New York at Dyckman's Oval, Fats was at the game. He used to play at the Lafayette Theater which was close to the Oval. When I say play, I mean play. That man could really tickle the ivories.

"Lionel Hampton used to hang around the games too. I guess out in Kansas City they made him an honorary coach and let him handle third base for awhile."

Once on the field, however, it was all business, and the blacks considered playing "tough" baseball as another important aspect of professionalism. Their concern for providing good role models and their interest in the refinements of the entertainment world, as well as feelings for friends, disappeared during a game. Aggressive, and sometimes vicious, baserunning made playing the infield a very dangerous occupation.

According to Dick Seay, the Crawfords' brilliant defensive second baseman, "The runners really went after the pivotman on a double play. Even if it was their mother, they'd try to run over her."

"Some guys even sharpened their spikes with a file," says Cool Papa. "Crush Holloway was one of them. I guess he wanted to be like Ty Cobb.

"Your job is to take out the shortstop or the second basemen when they're tryin' to turn the double play. I would try to hit the man, but never hurt him or spike him. But a lot of guys didn't care who they hurt. The infielder just had to prove he had enough guts to stay in there no matter what."

Most of the black pitchers threw at batters, brushing them back or resorting to flagrant knockdown pitches. "Cannonball Dick Redding would throw at anybody," said Judy Johnson. "It was scary because he was so big and he could throw as hard as anybody who ever played the game."

Lena Horne

Satchel Paige refused to throw at batters. "If the only way you could win was by busting a man's head or caving in his ribs," he said, "you shouldn't be too proud of yourself."

"I wasn't worried about pushing those big home run hitters off the plate. Fact is, I wasn't worried about them at all. The guys who handled the bat were the really tough hitters. Guys like Cool. He hit me pretty good when we went up against each other. The reason he did so well was that he used a half-swing. It's hard to throw a ball by a man who only takes a half-swing."

The aggressiveness and toughness also extended to the umpires. Players freely argued with the officials, cursed them, and even physically attacked them. The abuse became so bad that some umpires began carrying guns under their gear. "Oscar Charleston was one of the worst," said Judy Johnson. "He was mean even when he was younger, but when he was with the Crawfords, he got even worse. As he grew older, he grew nastier. One night at Greenlee Field, I saw him grab an umpire by the throat and threaten to throw him up in the stands. Luckily, we convinced him not to do it."

Barnstorming earned more black ink for Greenlee's baseball operation than playing in Pittsburgh. The Crawfords therefore spent much time on the road. Away from the comforts of home, and the acceptance of the black community, the hardships abounded. The team's brotherhood and professionalism provided the men with strength to endure and make sacrifices to play the game they loved, and to play it very well. Foremost among their problems was racism.

"I grew up in the South," says Cool Papa. "So, I know what prejudiced people can be like. Most of the bad things they do are because of the way they were brought up. They really don't know any better.

"Wherever the Crawfords played in the South, there were white people there at the game right along with the blacks. They always had to sit on opposite sides of a rope. A white man and a black man could be sitting right next to each other, but they had a rope between. Silly isn't it. But that's the way it was.

"Another time, I think it was during spring training, the Crawfords had played someplace in Mississippi and were on the way back to New Orleans. We had about twenty-five men with us, more than we normally carried during the regular season.

"We stopped at a colored restaurant in the little town of Picayune, Mississippi, and tried to get something to eat. 'Oh no,' said the people at the restaurant. "There are too many of you. It'll take us too long to fix food for so many.'

"The restaurant people came out and looked at our bus, and one of them said, 'Whose on this bus? Any white boys on there?'

'No,' we told them.

'Who owns it?'

'The Pittsburgh Crawfords baseball team. Can't you read the sign?'

'A colored baseball team?'

'Yes, colored.'

'Well,' they said, 'you all better get out of Mississippi as quick as you can.'

'Why?'

'Because if you don't, they're gonna take all you guys on this bus and put you working out on the farm.'

'Who's gonna put us on a farm?'

'The police, that's who. There's a lot of people out there on the farm right now they caught passing through. They jail people for speeding and then make them serve their sentence out on the farm. They love to catch colored folks.'

"Well, we got back on the bus right away. We drove straight through until we were out of the state of Mississippi.

"It's a good thing Satchel wasn't with us. He always traveled in his own car, you know. If he had been with us, there would have been trouble. Satchel was not a man to take racial things without fighting back. He would have challenged somebody.

"Sometimes, though, Satchel handled the situation with a little humor. One time, he was on his way to a game someplace in the South and got picked up for speeding. Knowing Satchel he probably was speeding. Anyway, he went up before the local judge and was fined forty dollars. Satch gave the judge eighty dollars and told him he was comin' through again the next day."

In another incident, Judy Johnson remembered a time when he and Ted Page found themselves facing a shotgun in a small southern town. "There were two guys and they told us they didn't like the way we were dressed. We were dressed pretty well, of course, and they said they didn't want any 'high falutin' niggers in their town. They told us to get out or they'd shoot us."

"Most of the time, when the Crawfords barnstormed in the small towns, it was really a big occasion for the people. They didn't really expect their local boys to beat a professional team like us, and everybody just had a good time.

"Once in a while, the people would get mad when we beat their boys. Sometimes it got real nasty. Once, they stopped the Crawfords' bus on the way out of town and charged the driver with running a red light and speeding. He hadn't done either, but the team secretary had to pay a big fine before we could leave town. Some people just have to get their revenge I guess.

"Another time after we beat a team in a small town, we stopped for something to eat. We got our food with no problem for a change, but then they charged us about ten times what it was worth. They said they'd call the cops if we didn't pay, so we gave them the money just to save trouble."

Ted Page in 1931.

Cool Papa remembers one game when the fans' anger became dangerous. "I don't remember exactly where it happened. I think it was someplace in Arkansas. Anyway, we were beating this team really bad, about 15–1 or so. Charleston liked to show people up and rub in it when he got the chance. He was on first, and Judy singled to right. Charleston headed for third and cut about 20 feet inside second base, laughing all the time. The umpires didn't notice and when Charleston was allowed to stay at third base, some of the people in the stands got real mad and started yelling, but we didn't think it would go any further.

"A couple of innings later, I was on deck, and somebody threw a chair down out of the stands at me. It just missed. Josh went up in the stands, which probably wasn't very smart. But he looked so powerful that nobody tried to do anything to him. He didn't find the guy either.

"After the game, I thought there was going to be a big fight. The crowd threatened us, but Charleston went nose-to-nose with the ringleader and backed him down. Of course, Charleston had some pretty strong backing with guys like Josh and Ted Page there. Ted wasn't scared of anybody."

Once back on the road, the hardships continued. The bus trips and the endless schedules wore the players down. "The idea," said Judy Johnson, "was for the Crawfords to make money. And the only way to make money was to play a lotta games. So when we were out on the road, they kept us on the move. We had a big Mack bus, just about the best Gus could buy, but it was still very tiring. I'll say this, though, Gus knew how it was for us because he went on some of the trips. He even drove once in a while."

"We used to play a night game on Saturday in one place," says Bell, "get on the bus and play a doubleheader someplace else on Sunday, and then play still another place on Sunday night. All the riding could be very uncomfortable. I was one of the first ballplayers, black or white, to wear glasses. On one of the bus trips, we hit a big bump. I was asleep and hit my head on the side of the bus. It messed up my eyesight, and I've worn glasses ever since. Gus wasn't too sure that wearing glasses was a good idea for a ball player, but I proved to him I could still do the job.

"We didn't play on the best of fields all the time either. It was great when we played in major league parks, but most of the time, we played on little more than playgrounds. The ground was hard and rough. I used to slide a lot, so I got strawberries all the time. The knees would be skinned on both sides from sliding. I would get sponges, cut holes out of them, and tape them around my knees to keep the uniform off the sore spots. It bothered me a lot, but like everybody else, I just had to keep goin'."

To keep going meant dealing with the problem of finding places to stay. Even when the Crawfords could find an establishment that allowed Negroes, the conditions were usually terrible. "Most of the time," said Ted Page, "we stayed in cabins at the edge of town. Today, you might call them motels, but they were just rough little cabins. Sometimes, we had to try and sleep with three or four guys in the bed, and sometimes we had to lay there with the lights on to keep the bedbugs from coming out."

Food and water could also be problems. Once, while Monte Irvin played for the Newark Eagles, the team stopped at a restaurant between Birmingham and Montgomery, Alabama. It was a very hot day and they simply wanted something to drink. As soon as they entered the restaurant, however, the owner began shaking her head no.

"Why are you saying no," one of the Eagles asked. "You don't even know what we want."

"Whatever you want, I don't have it," she replied.

"How about some soft drinks?" asked one of the players.

"No," she said.

"Could we have some well water? It's very hot."

The woman finally allowed the team to drink from her well. As the bus pulled away, however, they saw her smashing the drinking gourd to pieces.

Much of the time in the South, as well as in the North, the Crawfords couldn't find restaurants that served blacks. Therefore, in addition to providing transportation and sleeping quarters, the big Mack bus became a place for the men to eat sandwiches, apples, cantaloupes, and melons purchased from roadside stands.

Food could mean fun as well as sustenance. Jimmie Crutchfield remembers one of those times. "Everybody would put their food up on the rack while they were asleep. It was pretty common to swipe the food and pass it around. One night, Harry Kincannon, the pitcher, came on board with a nice bunch of fried chicken. "Tincan," as we called him, ate some of the chicken and then put it up. He was sure to let everybody see that he was carrying a little pistol, a gun which belonged to Charleston, who had picked it up from a politician in Cuba. Kincannon tried to threaten us by saying, 'Anybody who messes with my chicken will have to mess with this here gun.' Well, we didn't pay much attention to him, and when the gun fell on the floor while he was asleep, somebody picked it up and emptied out all the shells. Then we passed Tincan's chicken around. We ate the chicken and then somebody tied the bones in a necklace and put it around Tincan's neck. When he woke up, everybody howled. At first Tincan was mad, but then he started laughing at himself."

Dizzy Dean

The Crawfords also had fun playing against major leaguers. After the 1934 season, they played an exhibition game against a contingent of big leaguers led by Dizzy Dean, the zany right-hander of the world champion St. Louis Cardinals.

Dean first tasted Crawford medicine in York, Pennsylvania. Shortly before the game, he ambled over and did some pleading with his black friends. "I just pitched two days ago," he said. "My flipper's tired, so kinda take it easy on me."

"Sure, Diz, you know you can count on us," said Josh Gibson with a sly grin.

Bell and Ted Page opened the game with line-drive singles. Dean then filled the bases by walking Oscar Charleston. Next came Gibson, and Dizzy served him a high fastball. Josh's eyes lit up like a pinball machine and he smashed the fat bug high and far over the center field fence.

For once, the talkative Dean stood speechless. As the grinning Gibson circled the bases, he yelled, "Hey, Diz, I told ya that ya could count on us."

In the second inning, the Crawfords extended their lead to 8–0, and Dean refused to pitch any more, moving to second base. Meanwhile, Satchel fanned 16 of the first 18 men he faced, and Pittsburgh breezed to an 11–1 victory. "They batted by ear that day," Paige remembered. "They sure couldn't see the Long Tom."

Even though the victory over the Dean Stars seemed to leave little room for improvement, the black players discussed the game in great detail. "In the Negro League," said Satchel Paige, "the manager's job was to tell people about their mistakes and how they could correct them. It wasn't that way in the big leagues."

"On the bus," says Cool Papa, "people slept, ate, kidded around, sometimes sang, and spent a lotta time discussing baseball. We all loved the game and we had great pride in ourselves. We always wanted to do better and one of the best ways to get better is to discuss your mistakes and get advice from the other guys. We all pulled together and tried to help each other. I guess doing well was so important to us because we wanted to prove to the white men that we were good enough to play in the major leagues. We wanted to be ready when the time came. We knew it would come eventually.

"All through my career, we put emphasis on what I call tricky baseball. We tried to play with our heads more than with our muscles.

"When I was with the Crawfords, we had two of the greatest power hitters who ever played baseball in Josh Gibson and Oscar Charleston. Everybody appreciated what they could do with the bat, but we still played a game based on strategy and fundamentals like advancing the runner, bunting, stealing, taking the extra base, hitting the cut-off man, and throwing to the right base, all those things you need to do to win ball games and be a really great team.

"I think the reason we had so much success against major leaguers was the differences in styles. The major leaguers waited around for somebody to hit a home run, while we worked on the strategy and the fundamentals. Nobody did it better than the Crawfords either."

"Yes," says Jimmie Crutchfield, "those were great times with the Crawfords. Some of the greatest times of my life. I'm very proud to have played for the Pittsburgh Crawfords because we were a team both on and off the field. We won together and we lost together. We laughed together and we cried together. We just cared about each other. How could anything be any better than that?"

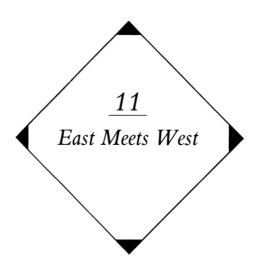

11

East Meets West

The East-West Game gave us the chance to show

our stuff to white society.

Willie Wells, Shortstop
Chicago American Giants

---

*A*rch Ward, the publicity-wise sports editor of the *Chicago Tribune,* conceived and promoted the first major league All-Star game. Played in Chicago's mammoth Comiskey Park on July 6, 1933, the contest featured the greatest white stars of the National and American Leagues. A massive advertising campaign by the *Tribune* billed the spectacle as "The Game of the Century."

Before 47,000 fans, the American League grabbed a 3–0 lead in the first three innings and cruised to a 4–2 victory. The New York Yankees contingent dominated, as Babe Ruth slammed a two-run homer and fastballing left-hander Lefty Gomez posted the victory.

Just over two months later, on September 10, Comiskey Park hosted black baseball's first East-West All-Star classic. Roy Sparrow, one of Gus Greenlee's employees, originated the idea in 1932. For 10 percent of the gate, Greenlee promoted the event, hiring Abe Saperstein of Harlem Globetrotter fame to handle the publicity. Despite a strong effort by Saperstein, the white press remained uninterested and uninformed about the event. Typically, the *Tribune's* brief advance read: "Colored Teams Play Today for Baseball Title."

For blacks, however, the game ranked as a happening of the first magnitude. It overshadowed the Black World Series because it involved the fans, whereas the series most often meant competition between the richest owners who like their contemporary counterparts, could afford the best players. The fans chose the All-Star teams and everyone had a chance to vote for personal favorites. The two largest black newspapers in the country, the *Chicago Defender* and the *Pittsburgh Courier,* conducted the voting. Players from these cities therefore dominated the squads.

Talent certainly abounded. Oscar Charleston topped the balloting with 43,973 votes. Much to Greenlee's pleasure, the fans selected seven other Crawfords for the East: Cool Papa Bell, Josh Gibson, Judy Johnson, second baseman John Henry Russell, pitchers Sam Streeter and Nat Hunter, and, of course, Satchel Paige. Paige declined to play, having a better financial offer to pitch a game in New York City. Two former Crawfords, Jud Wilson, called "Boojum" because of the sound of his line drives bouncing off the fence, and outfielder Rap Dixon, a man of speed and power, were also chosen.

In addition to Dixon, Wilson, and the Crawfords' contingent, the Eastern squad featured Biz Mackey of the Philadelphia Stars, the finest of defensive catchers; strong-armed shortstop Dick Lundy, also of the Philadelphia Stars; and outfield speedster Fats Jenkins of the New York Black Yankees.

The West countered with a talented group of their own, led by outfielder Turkey Stearnes, Willie Wells, first baseman Mule Suttles, and left-handed pitcher Willie Foster, all from the Chicago American Giants. Stearnes, a left-handed power hitter, rivaled Josh Gibson in long ball production. Wells, outstanding with the bat, also played a brilliant defensive shortstop. Suttles was another first class power hitter. Willie Foster, Rube's half-brother, stood as the best left-hander in black baseball. In addition to a blazing fastball, Foster threw a sharp-breaking curve, a sinker, and a baffling change-up. Each of these men, especially Stearnes and Wells, deserve consideration for the Hall of Fame.

For the fans, the East-West game meant glamour. The *Defender* called the occasion a "highlight in the affairs of the elite" and it provided a motive for many middle-class blacks to vacation in Chicago and stay at the Grand Hotel which housed the players. In fact, as ticket sales zoomed, during the days preceding the game, the Union Pacific placed additional cars on their Chicago-bound trains from Arkansas, Louisiana, Missouri, and Tennessee.

The morning of September 10th dawned dark and rainy. At game time, Chicago lived up to its name of the "Windy City." Strong winds puffed off Lake Michigan, lightning slashed the sky, and thunder boomed across the heavens. Despite the ominous weather, an enthusiastic early afternoon crowd gathered at Comiskey Park. An exuberant Al Monroe wrote in the *Defender,* "The Depression didn't stop 'em—the rain couldn't—and so a howling thundering mob of 20,000 souls braved an early downpour and a threatening storm to see the pick of the West's baseball players beat the pick of the East 11–7 in a Game of Games."

Willie Foster started for the West. Leading off for the East, speedboy Cool Papa Bell demonstrated his fine power from the right side. Foster delivered a sizzling letter-high fastball on the first pitch, and Bell wrist-snapped a towering drive into deep left field. "Steel Arm" Davis drifted to the wall and then gave up on the blast as a home run. Suddenly, a strong gust of wind pushed the ball back in the park where a surprised Davis made the catch.

Despite the tough break on Bell's drive, the East jumped off to an early lead, assisted by the West's second baseman, Leroy Morney, who booted three chances. "Leroy Morney," wrote Monroe, seemed to have been alone in thinking the balls were covered with moss that should not be removed."

The East led 3–1 in the bottom of the third, when little lefty Sam Streeter of the Crawfords faced powerful Mule Suttles with two runners on base. Over in the West's dugout, Willie Wells kept yelling, "Kick, Mule! Kick, Mule!" At 6′ 6″ and 230 pounds, he did kick. Streeter hung one of his spitters letter high and Suttles swatted the ball high and far into left field. The majestic drive soared out of the park between the grandstand and the roof, shattering a taxi window in a parking lot adjacent to Princeton Street. While the East bounced back with two runs in the top of the fifth, Wells and "Double Duty" Radcliffe doubled back-to-back in the bottom of the sixth to tie the score. Radcliffe had acquired his unusual nickname when he pitched the first game of a doubleheader and then caught the second. After Radcliffe came Mule again. Eastern Manager Dick Lundy pulled Streeter and replaced him with another Crawford, Nat Hunter. Suttles drilled Hunter's first offering for a single to drive home Radcliffe and give the West a lead it never relinquished.

Gus Greenlee, already unhappy with Satchel Paige for skipping the big game, found no pleasure in the performance of his Crawfords. They contributed little offense, while both Streeter and Hunter were hit hard, with Streeter suffering the loss.

Bell, Charleston, and Gibson made the East's team again in 1934, this time joined by fellow Crawfords, outfielder Jimmie Crutchfield, catcher Bill Perkins, outfielder Vic Harris, second baseman Chester Williams, and pitcher Harry Kincannon. This time, Satchel Paige joined them and dominated the contest.

Chester Washington of the *Pittsburgh Courier* set the stage for Satchel before the game began:

> If 30,000 attend, 29,999 will be hoping to see the slowmoving fastball-pitching Satchel (sic) Paige, hero of recent Denver Post Tourney, in action. "Satch," who won three games in five days out in the Mile High City, in addition to being a great speedball pitcher is one of the best natural showmen in baseball. He is to Negro baseball what Babe Ruth and Carl Hubbell were to the majors in yesteryears.

With the game scoreless in the seventh, Willie Wells doubled for the West with nobody out and Paige was summoned from the bullpen. Washington described the scene:

> Pandemonium spread in the West's cheering sections. An instant later a hush fell upon the crowd as the mighty Satchel Paige, prize "money" pitcher for the East, leisurely ambled across the field to the pitcher's box. It was a dramatic moment. Displaying his picturesque double wind-up and nonchalant manner, Satchel started shooting 'em across the plate, and in five tosses fanned Radcliffe. The East's supporters breathed a sigh of relief and Satchel settled to his task. "Turkey" Stearns flied out to Vic Harris and "Mule" Suttles' bat dropped another fly ball into the accurate hands of Harris. This sounded taps for the West, because from then on Sir Satchel was the master of the situation.

In his enthusiasm for Paige, Washington overlooked the contributions of Cool Papa Bell and his teammate in right field, Jimmie Crutchfield. With the score deadlocked at 0–0, Cool led off the eighth inning with a free pass and promptly stole second. After the next two batters failed to deliver, Jud Wilson slapped a ball into the shortstop hole and beat the long throw to first. Late in the game, with no score, Bell decided to gamble. Instead of stopping at third, he put on a burst of speed and roared towards home. Surprised, first baseman Suttles hesitated before throwing. It was a costly hesitation and Cool beat Larry Brown's tag with a beautiful hook slide, giving the East a 1–0 lead.

With one out in the bottom of the ninth, Suttles slashed a triple to left-center for his third hit of the day. Even with Satchel on the mound, the East's lead seemed in jeopardy as the powerful Red Parnell of the Nashville Elite Giants stepped to the plate. A nervous chill rippled through the East's supporters as Parnell casually knocked the dirt from his spikes and set himself to hit. Paige kicked high and delivered one of his Long Toms. A roar came from the stands as Parnell blistered a line drive to Crutchfield in deep right. As Crutch made the catch, Mule tagged up at third and tried to score. Crutchfield whipped a bullet throw all the way to the plate on the fly. Ball and runner arrived home at the same time, but Bill Perkins made a quick tag on the astonished Suttles for a game-ending double play.

In 1935 pitcher Leroy Matlock joined Bell, Charleston, Gibson, Crutchfield, and Williams on the Crawfords' contingent. This time, because of franchise changes, the Crawfords joined the Chicago American Giants on the Western squad.

The 1935 game ranks as the most exciting in the East-West series and Jimmie Crutchfield again provided the defensive gem. Cool Papa Bell recalls the play: "It was the top of the eighth, and Biz Mackey was up. He was a switch-hitter, and this time he was batting left-handed. He lined a ball into the right-center field gap between Jimmie and me. Both of us went after it, but neither of us could make the call. At the last second, Crutchfield cut in front of me, jumped way up in the air, and caught the ball in his meat hand. I never saw a better catch. I doubt if anyone ever saw a better catch." Kevin Mitchell, the San Francisco Giants left fielder, made a similar catch during the 1989 season.

Once more, however, Mule Suttles, batting against future Hall-of-Famer, Martin Dihigo, ignited the loudest fireworks of the day. Another *Courier* reporter, William Nunn, relived the excitement in Comiskey Park:

"For the West, Mule Suttles at bat!"
That's the resonant voice of the announcer, speaking through the new public address system of the park.
"T-H-E M-U-L-E!"

Martin Dihigo

Reverberating through the reaches of this historic ballpark and bounding and rebounding through the packed stands comes the chant of some 25,000 frenzied spectators.

They're yelling for blood! They're yelling for their idol, the bronzed Babe Ruth of colored baseball to come through.

It's more than a call! It's a chant! It's a prayer! Surely, that superb slugger out there, pitting his eyes against the blinding speed-ball of one of the greatest all-around ballplayers ever to tear up turf with pitching spikes, has heard the call! But let us show you the picture in its entirety.

Prior to the eleventh inning of the East-West classic, the East, underdogs of the game, had bared their fangs early to grip a lead only to see it melt into nothingness in the latter innings of the contest.

Through the ninth, the two teams had battled to a 4–4 stalemate. Into the tenth they had gone, and it was here that the East had made its "gesture supreme." Four times they had crossed the plate, to apparently pack the game away on ice.

And then, as in an Horatio Alger "hero book," the East, with their backs to the wall, had scored four times in their half of the tenth to even things again, 8–8.

Throughout the first half of the eleventh, the West had held the East scoreless. There were no more innings on the scorecard, and we'd gone over to another page.

Then came the last half of the eleventh.

Cool Papa Bell had worked Dihigo, who had come out of centerfield to pitch for the East, into a hole and had strolled to first base. Hughes went out, Dihigo to Dandridge on a perfect sacrifice as Bell streaked the other way scooting to the midway station.

Chester Williams was called out on strikes after vehemently insisting that one of Dihigo's blazing fastballs had hit him.

Josh Gibson, catching for the West, and who had connected for two doubles and two singles in five trips to the plate, was purposely shunted.

And that's the picture as the announcer's voice, rather hoarse from detailing eleven innings of superb competition, announced: "For the West, Suttles at bat."

Dihigo, his uniform dripping with perspiration, wiped the sweat out of his eyes, and shot a fastball across the plate. Ball one, said Umpire Craig.

Again, came that blinding fastball, letter high and splitting the plate. And the count was one and one.

Suttles stepped out of the batter's box, dried his sweating palms in the dust around home plate, tugged at his cap, and moved back into position. He looked dangerous as he wangled his big, black club around. But so did Dihigo, who was giving his all.

Once again came that smooth motion, that reflex action of the arm, and then! —a blur seeming catapult towards the plate.

Suttles threw his mighty body into motion. His foot moved forward. His huge shoulder muscles bunched. Came a swish through the air, a crack as of a rifle, and like a projectile hurled from a cannon, the ball started its meteoric flight. On a line it went. It was headed for right center. Bell and Gibson were away with the crack of the bat. But so was Arnold, centerfielder of the East team and Ohms, dependable and dangerous Cuban star, who patrolled the right garden. No one thought the ball would carry to the stands.

Headed as it was, it took a drive of better than 450 feet to clear the fence.

The ball continued on its course and the packed stands rose to their feet. Was it going to be caught? Was it going to hit the stand?

No folks! That ball, ticketed by Mule Suttles, CLEARED the distant fence in far away right center, landing 475 feet from home plate. It was a herculean swat. One of the greatest in all baseball. As cheering momentarily hushed in the greatest tribute an athlete can ever receive, we in the press box heard it strike the back of a seat with a resounding thud, and then go bounding merrily on its way.

And then . . . pandemonium broke loose. Suttles completed his trip home, the third-base line filled with playmates anxious to draw him to their breasts. Over the stands came a surging mass of humanity.

Furthermore, according to the *Defender:*

Score cards were torn up and hurled into the air. Men tossed away their summer straw hats, and women screamed.

Mule was less successful at a dance staged in his honor that night. Resplendent in a white suit, and attempting to draw the attention of an attractive young lady, he jumped from the balcony to the dance floor. The band played for him, but the girl, refusing his offer to dance, said, "If you're strong enough to jump off the balcony, what would you do to my feet if you stepped on them. No thank you!"

Left-hander Leroy Matlock of the Crawfords picked up the pitching victory in the 1936 game, again supported by a large group of his teammates: Bell, who had a big day with three hits, Gibson, Crutchfield, Paige, outfielder Sam Bankhead, first baseman John Washington, and Judy Johnson, who returned to the game after a two-year absence. During the 1934 and 1935 games, Greenlee had dispatched the dependable Johnson with barnstorming teams to earn extra dollars for the Crawfords' treasury.

The Crawfords' downhill slide began in 1937, and only Chester Williams, catcher Pepper Bassett, and pitcher Barney Morris made the Eastern team. During the Crawfords' final year in 1938, pitcher Schoolboy Johnny Taylor was their sole representative.

Beginning in 1941, the East-West classic became a showcase for players being scouted by major league teams. In that year, future major leaguers and future Hall-of-Famers Monte Irvin and Roy Campanella played for the East, and through the

Josh Gibson

final contest in 1950, Joe Black, Larry Doby, Junior Gilliam, Sam Jethroe, Minnie Minoso, Jackie Robinson, and others used the game as a stepping stone to the big leagues. Jackie Robinson, of the Kansas City Monarchs, played shortstop for the West in 1945, and went 0–5 at the plate.

David Malarcher, a star infielder, and later manager of the Chicago American Giants, believed the East-West classic provided not only the showcase, but also the impetus for baseball integration. "Branch Rickey," he said, "was more interested in business than social reform. When we drew around 50,000 fans for each East-West game from 1941 through 1944, he knew black fans would pay to see good baseball. Pay was the word. He also knew that black talent could help bring some pennants to Brooklyn. He then signed Jackie Robinson to a contract in 1945."

The vibrant memories of Comiskey Park came alive once more on July 6, 1983, when the Chicago White Sox hosted an Old-Timers game, preceding by just one day the 50th anniversary of the first white All-Star game. Before the crowd thrilled again to the special grace and charm of Brooks Robinson, and saw Sweet Billy Williams drive a ball into the upper deck, three dark old men walked to home plate. Judy Johnson and Cool Papa Bell, arm-in-arm, watched with pride as Willie Wells threw out the first ball. For one beautiful moment, black and white All-Stars of the past stood tall and proud, bonded by the game they loved.

12

An Island Away from Home

It was kinda scary down there in the Dominican Republic. Too many secrets. Too many police and soldiers with guns. Those voodoo people. I was makin' good money, so I stayed to the end, but Ol' Satch was glad to get back home.

Satchel Paige, 1980
Springfield, Illinois

*M*any major leaguers played south of the border because it marked them as hardworking to spend their winter perfecting skills or keeping in shape. Minor leaguers, hoping for a major league job, played winter ball for the same reasons.

For American black players, a winter season in Cuba, Puerto Rico, Mexico, Panama, Venezuela, or in special situations, like the Dominican Republic, meant economic survival. They made so little money in black baseball that the thought of an off-season, or a vacation, was ridiculous. Some competed in California or Texas during the early winter season, but Latin America provided the most reliable source of income.

Besides the need for money, the absence of a color line in Latin America appealed to American blacks. They played with whites, Cubans, Puerto Ricans, and Mexicans before Latin crowds. Beyond understandable national loyalties, race made little difference.

While race failed to ignite their emotions, the Latin fans, often called "franticos," showed great compassion for the game. They loved American black stars and the foreign owners offered substantial salaries to keep the "Norteamericanos" coming back every winter.

Most of the time, the fans enhanced the appeal of Latin America for the blacks. As Willie Wells said about playing in Mexico, "We have everything first class here, plus the fact that people here are much more considerate than the American baseball fans. I mean that we are heroes here, and not just ballplayers."

In Cuba and Mexico, the fans gambled in the stands and sometimes rewarded an exceptional performance by throwing money to a player. "One time down in Mexico," Cool Papa Bell remembers, "I hit two inside-the-park homers in one game. After the second one, they threw pesos to me. It took a long time to pick them all up, but there was a lotta money."

The franticos' emotions could also be dangerous. While whistling signified disapproval, the spectators often went beyond this rather mild form of protest, screaming in Spanish at each other and the players. Home fans sometimes bombarded rival teams with lemons, oranges, and even the contents of bedpans.

Still, in the minds of most American black players, the benefits of Latin baseball far outweighed the negatives. In addition to the attractive salaries, the absence of racism, and the near hero worship of the fans, travel was minimal in comparison to the United States. Perhaps best of all, the lack of discrimination allowed a lifestyle that the black men found absolutely intoxicating. They could live anywhere, eat anywhere, and go anywhere. Furthermore, they had the money to enjoy their freedom.

The Dominican Republic, unlike some of the other Latin American countries, remained an unknown quantity to American players. During the late 1800s and early 1900s, the country experienced significant economic growth, but also substantial growth in its foreign debt. By an agreement concluded in 1905, the United States assumed control of the collection of Dominican customs duties and retained that power until 1941.

In 1916, after many attempts to pacify the various Dominican political groups, President Woodrow Wilson sent the U.S. Marines to occupy the violent-ridden nation. The occupation resulted in further economic development, with progress in both education and public health. It also resulted in military rule, press censorship, and economic exploitation by U.S. business interests. After U.S. forces were withdrawn in 1924, the country returned to political anarchy.

Rafael Leonidas Trujillo Molina, a military officer trained by the occupation forces, seized control of the presidency in 1930 during a time of extreme political and economic crisis. The Trujillo administration fostered political stability and economic growth. It also established a network of both public and private corruption. Allowing no political opposition, strongman Trujillo solidified a dictatorship in which he alone approved all public officials.

Santo Domingo, nearly destroyed by a hurricane a few months after Trujillo came to power, was restored and named Ciudad Trujillo. The dictator reorganized and modernized sugar, coffee, and cocoa plantations, placing them under the personal control of his family.

In time, many people came to resent the Trujillo administration and, despite the dictators' strong-arm techniques, substantial opposition arose early in 1937. Baseball in the Dominican was played in a league with teams representing Ciudad Trujillo, Santiago, and San Pedro de Macoris. Trujillo's two opponents backed the other teams, so it became quite important for Ciudad Trujillo to win the championship. Victory meant considerable enhancement for the winning sponsors' political reputation.

Trujillo initated an effort to bring the best black players to Ciudad Trujillo. Realizing the importance of pitching, Satchel Paige stood at the top of his list. He sent representatives to the United Sates to entice the big fireballer with large sums of money.

Satchel's defection to Bismarck hurt him with Gus Greenlee and with the entire black baseball establishment. He was considered an independent, irresponsible individual who would jump a contract with little hesitation. Even though a lone wolf, Satchel cared enough about his reputation to resist the initial advances of Trujillo's men.

In New Orleans, where the Crawfords held spring training, Satchel ducked the Trujillos time after time. One day, they trailed the elusive pitcher to his hotel and when he tried to escape in his car, their chauffeur blocked him with a big

The 1937 Trujillo All-Stars
Standing—Far left—Josh Gibson
                Fourth from left—Rudolpho
                Fernandez
                Sixth from left—Perucho Cepeda
                Far right—Bill Perkins
Middle—Dr. Jose Enrique Ayubar
                To His Left—Satchel Paige
Seated—Second from left—Leroy Matlock
                Fourth from left—Cool Papa Bell
                Fifth from left—Sam Bankhead

black limousine. Satchel explained that he didn't want to jump again, but when they showed him a gun and piles of greenbacks, they finally convinced him to pitch in the Dominican Republic.

Needing more players, the Trujillos asked Satchel to recruit several of his teammates, especially Leroy Matlock, Josh Gibson, and Cool Papa Bell. Leaving nothing to chance, Frederico Nina, one of Trujillo's men, followed the Crawfords back to Pittsburgh trying to recruit players. The entire black community, including Gus Greenlee and Oscar Charleston, became furious with the intruding Dominicans. Greenlee even went to the State Department in Washington seeking a way to stop the Dominicans from raiding his club.

"At first, even though we knew Satchel was going down to the Dominican Republic, we ignored the Trujillos," says Cool Papa Bell. "Then, the Crawfords fell on bad times and Greenlee stopped paying us. We needed money to support ourselves and our family, so we started thinking about the situation.

"I still didn't want to talk to the Trujillos because I didn't trust them. I was looking for somewhere to go when Satchel called me on the phone. 'We're in trouble down here,' he said. 'We're supposed to win the championship and I want some of you boys to come down. They'll give you $800, transportation, and all expenses for six weeks. How about it?'

"No, I told him. But make it $1000 and I'll say yes.

"Satchel put the head man on the phone, and he said yes to the $1000. Then I asked him for some of the money in advance.

" 'No' he said, 'we can't give you any money in advance.'

"I have to have some money before I leave, I said.

"He said he'd have to call me back and when he did, he said they'd give me $500 in Miami on the way down. 'We'll also have $500 for Gibson, Matlock, and anybody else you think can help the club. Our consul in Miami will meet your plane and give you the money.'

"I convinced Josh, Matlock, and Bankhead to come with me. They were a little doubtful, but decided to come along because I was in on it.

"Well, we did get our money in Miami, but when we got to Ciudad Trujillo, Satchel came to greet us with a bunch of soldiers carrying rifles and wearing bandoliers. I wondered just what I had gotten us into and the other guys were looking at me kinda funny."

"I said to Satch, 'what's goin' on here.' He just said, 'wait an' see.' "

Escorted to an impressive governmental building, the players were greeted by Dr. Jose Enrique Ayubar, Deputy of the National Congress and Dean of the National University. He had called a press conference and proceeded to introduce the players.

Following the introductions, Ayubar turned to a more pressing problem. Many of the country's people lived in poverty and resented so much money being spent on baseball. Dr. Ayubar tried to suppress the criticism.

"The money," Ayubar began, "was subscribed voluntarily by the enthusiastic baseball fans of this district. Neither the president of the republic, Dr. Rafael Trujillo, nor the government had to intervene in the importation of players.

"Baseball in Trujillo City is not commercial. Money makes no difference. Baseball, as indulged by the Latin races, is spiritual in every respect."

Many of the reporters began grinning at each other. Some just laughed out loud.

"The importation of colored American players resulted from a desire on the part of the provinces to win," Ayubar continued. "The Americans accepted the terms offered because the pay was much higher than that they were accustomed to receive in the Negro National League.

"They did not come by force, nor because they had been ousted from the league in the States. They came voluntarily. We would have imported American white players if the salaries of the white players had not been such that it was impossible for us to better them.

"This has been the biggest year in baseball ever seen here, because of peace, unity, and goodwill brought to the republic by President Trujillo, which accounts for the fact that the Dominican people do not wish him to leave office.

"American baseball magnates, however, need not fear a repetition of what happened this year. If baseball is played here next year, it will be during the winter and spring months."

Later, at a picnic at the presidential plantation, a reporter told Satch and Cool, "Trujillo runs everything down here, and he must win the championship. You see, his chief rivals have the other teams in the league. Trujillo will be very angry if you lose to those other teams."

According to Cool Papa, "They kept us under guard at a private club. There were men with guns around all the time. We could leave the club only two days a week. I don't know if they were trying to protect us or keep us from getting away. I do know that one of the guards told me, 'If you don't win they're going to kill Trujillo.'

"I laughed and said, they don't kill people over baseball games."

"He didn't laugh. He looked me right in the eye and said, 'Down here, they will do it.' "

Chet Brewer, the star black hurler imported by one of the other politicos to pitch for Santiago, went looking for Satchel one day so they could share a few beers. Brewer couldn't find Paige, and knowing the small boys of the Latin towns knew all the business, he asked one of them were to find Satch. According to Brewer, the boy told him, "He's in el carcel, the jail. They're not afraid of him trying to get away, they're afraid somebody might try to shoot him."

"We really had a pretty good time down there," says Bell, "at least while we were at the club. We had the ocean for swimming and fishing. We played a lotta cards. It was just real relaxing, something we weren't used to."

Outside, the pressure to win was intense. After losing a series to Santiago, the Trujillo team returned to the club, only to be confronted by a group of angry soldiers. "El Presidente doesn't lose," they shouted while firing their rifles in the air.

Having fun in the Dominican are Cool Papa
Bell, with Leroy Matlock over his shoulder,
and Satchel Paige in the background.

"Playing the games was tough," says Bell. "People tried everything to win and
to get an advantage. The first time I hit a triple, they stopped the game and argued
that I must have cut across the infield. It was impossible for me to have gotten to
third base so fast. They argued for about 10 minutes but they finally let me keep
third base.

"You know, on our Trujillo club we had some great ballplayers. Satch. Josh.
Bankhead. Bill Perkins, another Crawford that Satchel convinced to come down.
Perucho Cepeda, "El Toro," from Puerto Rico. Rudopho Fernandez, one of the
best pitchers in Cuba. Even with all these guys, we went down to the last day to
decide the championship. Just shows you how good the competition was there."

Satchel Paige received most of the attention from both those who wanted Trujillo to win and those who wanted Trujillo to lose. "Haiti is more or less west of
the Dominican Republic," Satchel recalled, "and that's where they have all those

voodoo people. Well, some of them came over into the Dominican of course. One of them gave me a magic charm called a caprelata, or something like that, which was supposed to help us win. Another one of them gave me a wanga and it was also supposed to help us win. Later, I found out that the wanga was really an evil charm to bring us bad luck. I just didn't want to have very much to do with those spirit people."

Just before the championship game, Dr. Ayubar spoke to the Ciudad Trujillo team. "You must win," he said.

"What do you mean, we must win?" Satchel asked.

"I mean exactly what I said," replied Ayubar. "Please take my advice and win. If you don't, you may never see America again."

Paced by Chet Brewer's strong arm and big bat, Santiago led Ciudad Trujillo 3–2 going into the bottom of the seventh inning. According to Paige, "You could see Trujillo lining up his army along the sidelines. The Santiago men were on the other side of the field. They looked like firing squads."

"Chet Brewer was tough that day," says Cool Papa. "Really he was tough every time you faced him. He had great stuff and he cut the ball besides."

"I singled with two outs in the seventh. Sammy Bankhead was coming up and I wanted to get in scoring position. We needed the run to tie it up. Brewer threw over to first a whole lot of times, but I still got a good jump and stole it fairly easy."

"Brewer tried to be real careful with Bankhead because he knew the man was a great clutch hitter. Well, he got a little too careful, and the count went to 3 and 1. Brewer came in with some smoke, but he got it up high. Bankhead had a tremendous cut but fouled it back. When I saw the pitch, I thought Bankhead would drive it, so I was real disappointed. But on 3 and 2, Bankhead connected. He was a line-drive hitter, and this one went on a line and just kept rising until it went way over the left-field fence. Boy was I happy and so were all the other guys."

As usual, Satchel rose to the occasion and retired the next six batters in order, five of them on strikes. "I don't think I ever threw harder," he said.

That evening, Trujillo threw a lavish party to celebrate the championship. Unfortunately, the beauty of the glorious sunset, framed by palm trees, was marred by the ominous presence of stern-faced soldiers carrying machine guns.

The next morning, the American players boarded a Pam Am Clipper for the island-hopping trip back to the United States. They carried their uniforms with them, and upon returning home, launched a successful barnstorming tour as the Trujillo All-Stars, concluding with a victory in the prestigious *Denver Post* Tournament.

Cool Papa Bell says, "I guess we saved Trujillo's life that time. But they assassinated him about 25 years later."

"Everybody back in the States was mad at us because they believed we ran out on Gus Greenlee. I can't speak for the other guys, but I needed the money. I had to go somewhere to earn a living."

A combination of things finished the Crawfords. When we left, the team was already in financial trouble and probably wouldn't have survived even if we had stayed. On the other hand, our leaving speeded up the end and left no hope for the team's survival. The biggest drawing cards, Satch and Josh, were gone. They still had Charleston and Crutchfield, but Charleston was just about over the hill and they traded Crutchfield. Also, when they traded Judy Johnson he retired. We left before the 1937 season and the team lasted through 1938, but they had little success.

"I felt sorry for Gus and I talked to him several years later about having left the team. He said he understood. The club was losing money and it was best for him to get out of baseball at the time. It was still too bad, because the Crawfords were the best."

13
The Chosen One

I've seen the bloody battlefields, and if black men can fight and die in Okinawa, Guadalcanal, and in the South Pacific, they can play baseball in America.

A. B. "Happy" Chandler
Hall of Fame Baseball Commissioner

During 1945, rumors spread about the impending integration of major league baseball. Most often mentioned to be the chosen one were outfielder Monte Irvin, whom the black veterans considered their best young player, and Jackie Robinson, the shortstop of the Montreal Royals.

Following a brilliant athletic career at UCLA, Robinson spent three years in the Army and then joined the Royals in 1945 for a salary of $400 a month. He had a good year, hitting .345, with 10 doubles, 4 triples, and 5 home runs in 41 games. He was voted as the West's starting shortstop in the East-West game.

Despite Robinson's impressive performance, the black veterans worried about his ability to succeed as a shortstop. They feared it might be a long time before another chance came along.

"One night," says Cool Papa Bell, "the Grays were playing the Monarchs in Wilmington, Delaware. Dizzy Dismukes, the Monarchs' road secretary came to me before the game and said, 'I think they're going to sign Robinson, but he wants to play shortstop. He can make it at first base, second base, or third base, but he can't go to his right and make the long throw from the shortstop hole. We've got to convince him to play another position.' "

"Dismukes asked me to hit the ball to Jackie's right during the game and force him to try and throw me out from the hole. Now, I was the kind of hitter who could hit the ball where I wanted nine times out of ten. So the first time I hit the pitch to Jackie's right and he got to the ball. But you can't take an extra step; you have to catch it and throw right away. Jackie had to take two steps and I beat his throw easy. Then I stole second. He caught the ball and I just slid under him. The next time up, I hit another ball to his right and beat the throw. I stole second again. This time I slid by the base and then reached back and tagged it. I walked two other times and followed with steals. I stole four bases even though my legs were bad and the throws were beating me to the bag."

"After the game, I went over to Robinson. He was mad and didn't want to talk to me. I finally got him to listen. I told him that I had purposely hit the ball to his right to show him he would be better off playing another position. I also told him he had to work on his tagging technique and learn to move his hands because those guys in the big leagues would go right around him just like I did. He did move to other infield positions as you know, and he learned how to handle tags too."

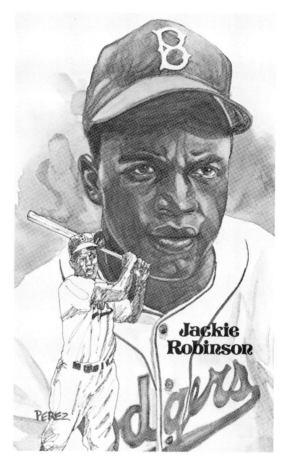

Jackie Robinson

Despite any worries the black players might have had, Wesley Branch Rickey, the bespectacled cigar-smoking general manager of the Brooklyn Dodgers, had already made up his mind. Rickey came to the Dodgers from the St. Louis Cardinals' front office in 1943. As he had done in St. Louis, he established a strong farm system to fuel the Dodger powerhouse. This time, however, he looked beyond the farm system for talent. His gaze focused on the wealth of available black baseball players.

Rickey moved to integrate baseball primarily because he wanted Brooklyn to become both a successful and prosperous franchise. A complex man, however, he

Branch Rickey

did express some humanitarian considerations. "I couldn't face my God any longer," he said, "knowing that his black children were held separate and distinct from white children in a game that has given me all I own."

He also remembered a moving experience during his tenure as baseball coach at Ohio Wesleyan University in the early 1900s. "A hotel in South Bend, Indiana, refused a room to my black catcher, Charles Thomas. The young man looked at his hands and cried, 'Black skin. If only I could make them white.' I promised myself that someday I would answer that cry."

Backed by the Dodgers' owners, and standing on high moral ground, Rickey went about the business of finding the right black player to integrate the game. Fearing great controversy during his preliminary moves, Rickey disguised the scouting of black players by announcing the formation of a black team called the Brooklyn Brown Dodgers, who would play in Ebbetts Field when the big club was on the road. Oscar Charleston would manage the team.

The Brown Dodgers joined the United States Baseball League, the brainchild of Gus Greenlee who in 1938 had folded his Crawfords and resigned from the NNL presidency. In addition to the Brown Dodgers and the new Crawfords, the league included teams from Chicago, Philadelphia, Detroit, and Toledo. The new league collapsed after just two months.

The failure of the United States League forced Rickey to revise his plans. But speculation remains as to just what constituted those plans. Did he really need the United States League for scouting purposes, or was it simply a mechanism through which Brooklyn could share the Negro League money with their New York City counterparts, the Yankees and the Giants? After all, the New York Black Yankees used Yankee Stadium and the New York Cubans used the Polo Grounds. Both major league teams reaped substantial profits from these arrangements.

Whatever his intentions, Rickey signed Jackie Robinson to a Brooklyn contract in the summer of 1945. Robinson, of course, went on to have a brilliant 1946 season with Brooklyn's Montreal Royals farm club in the International League. He followed this in 1947 with a season that led to his selection by *The Sporting News* as the National League's Rookie of the Year.

Branch Rickey provided a great service to baseball and to America by signing Jackie Robinson and then supporting him with steadfast courage through dangerous and trying times. Financial success, however, clearly remained his major objective. Still, Rickey accepted lifelong applause for his great humanitarianism.

Despite the controversy over his intentions, many of the black players revered Rickey for his efforts. According to Cool Papa Bell, however, they didn't demonstrate their respect. "When Branch Rickey died," he says, "I was very sad because he did a lot to help my people. Rickey's family asked Jackie Robinson to be one of the honorary pallbearers at the funeral, and Robinson asked me to be the other. I was honored to do it, but I was very angry the day we carried him. Besides Jackie and myself, Frank Duncan, the old Kansas City Monarchs' catcher, was the only other black person there. We should have given Mr. Rickey more respect, but I guess some of our people just didn't want to make the effort."

Far more deserving of accolades was Baseball Commissioner Happy Chandler, who began his term on November 1, 1945, approximately nine months after the death of his predecessor, Judge Kenesaw Mountain Landis. Landis had made little

Happy Chandler

effort to disguise his racial prejudice during his twenty-five years in office and stood as an unrelenting foe of integration. Hoping to acquire some political clout, and perhaps hoping another man of the South might continue the Landis legacy, the owners appointed Chandler.

As a former Governor of Kentucky, and at that time a United States Senator from the Bluegrass State, the owners did obtain some political power, but Chandler was no Landis. Instead, the new commissioner seemed eager to overcome the Landis legacy of hatred. At his first press conference, Chandler told reporters, "I'm for the four freedoms. I've seen the bloody battlefields, and if black men can fight

Kenesaw Mountain Landis

and die in Okinawa, Guadalcanal, and in the South Pacific, they can play baseball in America. I'm not running for anything right now, but I'm not running away from anything either, so when I give my word, you can count on it."

Chandler had given the green light and, of course, Branch Rickey proceeded. When it became apparent that Rickey wanted Jackie Robinson in Brooklyn for the 1947 season, a special committee composed of National League President Ford Frick, American League President Will Harridge, Tom Yawkey of the Boston Red Sox, Sam Breadon of the St. Louis Cardinals, Phillip Wrigley of the Chicago

Cubs, and Larry McPhail, of the New York Yankees prepared a secret report for the major league owners urging continuation of segregation. All of the copies of the report, except Chandler's, were destroyed. He released it to the public many years later.

The owners voted 15–1 against the transferral of Robinson's contract to Brooklyn, and Rickey cast the only positive vote. Ignoring the owner's mandate, the gutsy Chandler approved the transfer anyway, thereby making lifelong enemies and leading to his ouster from the commissionership in 1951.

Later, when Rickey came to visit him at home in Kentucky, Chandler explained his action. "Branch," he said, "someday I'm going to meet my maker. If he had to ask me why I wouldn't let a black man play, what could I tell him? Because of his color? That might not be a good enough answer.

"You know, Branch, the Negro Leagues have some of the finest players who ever stepped on a diamond. I feel sorry for Satchel Paige, Josh Gibson, Cool Papa Bell, Buck Leonard, and those other fellows who are already too old. Satchel once told me, 'If you'd been commissioner earlier, I'd have won 30 games for 30 years in the big leagues.'

"I saw the Homestead Grays play when they had Josh Gibson and Buck Leonard. I also saw the Pittsburgh Crawfords. They had quite a team with Paige, Gibson, Bell, and Oscar Charleston. I think Ty Cobb and Charleston were the two finest players I ever saw."

Chandler, of course, relished Jackie Robinson's success. He, like many Americans, considered baseball the greatest of all American institutions and the most beloved and honored of our sports. Unfortunately, until Robinson, the game perpetuated a myth of democracy in which equality prevailed. Robinson turned the myth into reality and allowed America to hold its head higher. Because of his monumental effort, America and baseball emerged in real sunshine, escaped some of the dark shadows of racism, and began keeping the promise of justice for all.

As a pathfinder athlete, Robinson opened the doors of major league baseball for generations of gifted black men. As early as 1947, owner Bill Veeck of the Cleveland Indians, courageous and innovative like Rickey, signed Newark Eagle's second baseman Larry Doby as the first black in the American League. Many others followed from the Negro Leagues, including Satchel Paige, Ernie Banks, and Hank Thompson of the Kansas City Monarchs; Hank Aaron of the Indianapolis Clowns (recommended by Oscar Charleston); Willie Mays of the Birmingham Black Barons; Roy Campanella, Joe Black, and Junior Gilliam of the Baltimore Elite Giants; Monte Irvin and Don Newcombe of the Newark Eagles; Minnie Minoso of the New York Cubans; and Sam Jethroe of the Cleveland Buckeyes.

Monte Irvin

Despite Jackie Robinson's aloofness from the Negro leaguers, the veteran black players supported him as a man. They admired the courage he displayed in surviving the intense racial pressures of his first seasons with the Dodgers and they admired the way he played the game. As Jimmie Crutchfield says, "Robinson was a fierce competitor. He put his heart and soul into baseball and developed into a great ballplayer."

Buck Leonard agrees with Crutchfield. "Robinson," he says, "turned out to be a wonderful player despite what he had to go through. Maybe Monte Irvin might have done what he did, and I know a few other guys who probably would have been successful, but they were already too old. So all in all, I think Jackie Robinson was the right man to integrate baseball."

Cool Papa Bell heard about the signing of Jackie Robinson while at home in St. Louis listening to his radio. "I cried because I was so happy," he says. "I'm proud to be in the Hall of Fame, but the best thing that ever happened for me in baseball was Jackie's signing.

"Robinson was just like Satchel, he believed he could do anything. I think he was at his best as a base runner. He stole about 200 bases in his career, including home 19 times. But it just wasn't the steals, he could upset a whole game by getting on base. He always kept the pitcher and catcher guessing. Always doing something to upset them."

These were bittersweet times for the black veterans. They watched with pride as the youngsters they trained moved into organized baseball. At the same time, they were saddened by the demise of their league. In 1947, as the black fans began to focus on Jackie Robinson and the black players in the minors, Negro League attendance plummeted and, with the exception of the New York Cubans and the Cleveland Buckeyes, all the teams lost money.

The next year proved even worse. Negro league teams did well to draw 2,000 even in major league parks, and attendance sometimes fell below 1,000. When the New York Black Yankees and the Newark Eagles folded at the end of the season, the Negro National League died, ending 16 years of continuous operation begun by Gus Greenlee in 1933.

A few black teams, while losing money at the gate, survived for a short time by selling players to organized baseball. The Chicago Cubs paid the top price of $30,000 to the Kansas City Monarchs for the contract of shortstop Ernie Banks. Three other men commanded a price of $15,000: pitcher Dan Bankhead of the Memphis Red Sox, purchased by the Brooklyn Dodgers; infielder Lorenzo "Piper" Davis of the Birmingham Black Barons, purchased by the Boston Red Sox; and a promising young outfielder named Willie Mays of the Birmingham Black Barons.

Before long, big league clubs began signing prospects directly from high school, thus eliminating black teams as middlemen. The Negro American League, composed of the Kansas City Monarchs, the Detroit-New Orleans Stars, the Birmingham Black Barons, and the Raleigh, North Carolina, Tigers, survived until 1960, primarily by barnstorming in small towns. The Indianapolis Clowns, a baseball burlesque show, lasted until 1968, and with their collapse, the last vestige of the once great Black Baseball Leagues disappeared. Thus ended a glorious chapter in American history.

14
Cherished Memories

Negro league players of the earlier decades
unfortunately were not recipients of enormous
commercial residuals and bonuses. We played for
something greater that could not be measured in
dollars and cents. The secrets of our game were to
enjoy and endure.

Judy Johnson, 1981
Wilmington, Delaware

*T*he men of the Crawfords loved to play baseball. When their careers ended, the best of times also ended. So as each ran off the field for the last time, the autumn leaves began to fall. They endured, sustained by their memories, and most did so with grace and dignity. Some have passed away, while others live in the deep winter of their time.

Big Red

The 1937 and 1938 seasons proved to be disasters for the Pittsburgh Crawfords both on the field and at the box office, so Gus Greenlee folded the team. Then, as black baseball rose to its financial zenith in the 1940s, he tried to return his Crawfords to the league. Now, however, the other owners no longer needed Big Red's financial support and they shut him out. His United States Baseball League, even with the support of Branch Rickey, failed miserably.

Late in 1938, Greenlee Field underwent the indignity of demolition; however, Gus carried on the great tradition of the Crawford Grille until 1950, when he suffered a serious stroke. He spent five weeks in the Veterans Administration Hospital in Aspinwall, Pennsylvania and, when he returned home, he needed full-time care. He also faced an Internal Revenue suit for back taxes. The Grille burned to the ground in 1951, but Gus was never told of the disaster. He died at his home on July 7, 1952.

Hall of Fame

Perhaps the most important event in the lives of some of the Crawford stars was their enshrinement in the Baseball Hall of Fame in Cooperstown, New York. Sadly, some died in the shadows, unaware of their recognition as one of baseball's greatest.

During his 1966 induction speech at Cooperstown, Ted Williams initiated the process by which pre-Jackie Robinson blacks would be elected to the Hall. He said:

> Inside this building are plaques dedicated to the baseball men of all generations. I'm privileged to join them. Baseball gives every American boy a chance to excel, not just be as good as someone else, but be better than someone else. This is the nature of man and the name of the game. I've been

Buck Leonard of the Homestead Grays.

a very lucky guy to have worn a baseball uniform, to have struck out or hit a tape-measure home run. I hope that someday the names of Satchel Paige and Josh Gibson in some way can be added as a symbol of the great Negro players that are not here only because they were not given the chance.

From this eloquent beginning, and the efforts of many others, including the late Dick Young of *The New York Daily News;* Bob Broeg, the former sports editor of *The St. Louis Post-Dispatch;* and the great Dizzy Dean, the Hall of Fame appointed a special Negro League Committee to choose the most deserving players. The Master, was first, elected in 1971. Paige was followed by Josh Gibson and Buck Leonard in 1972; Monte Irvin in 1973; Cool Papa Bell in 1974; Judy Johnson in 1975; Oscar Charleston in 1976; and John Henry Lloyd and Martin Dihigo in 1977. After the disbandment of the Negro League Committee, the Veteran's Committee, composed almost entirely of white men, elected Rube Foster in 1981 and the great third baseman Ray Dandridge in 1987.

Satch

Satchel's place in the limelight certainly continued after he left the St. Louis Browns in 1953. In fact, his fame grew. When he pitched his first game for the Miami Marlins in 1956, he flew into the stadium in a helicopter and sat on the sidelines in a rocking chair. His appearance that day in the Orange Bowl set a minor league attendance record of 51,713.

Whitey Herzog, in his book *White Rat,* discusses several of his experiences with Satchel during their time together with the Marlins:

> The Marlins once had a distance-throwing contest before a night game. Landrum and I had the best arms of any of the outfielders. We were out by the center-field fence, throwing two-hoppers to the plate. Ol' Satch came out, didn't even warm up, and kind of flipped the ball sidearm. It went 400 feet on a dead line and hit the plate. I wouldn't believe it if I hadn't seen it.
>
> We were on the road in Rochester one night, screwing around in the outfield. They had a hole in the outfield fence just barely big enough for a baseball to go through, and the deal was that any player who hit a ball through there on the fly would win $10,000. I started trying to throw the ball through the hole, just to see if I could do it. I bet I tried 150 or 200 times, but I couldn't do it, so I went back to the dugout.
>
> When Satch got to the park I said 'Satch, I bet you can't throw the ball through that hole out there.'
>
> He looked out at it and said, 'Wild Child, do the ball fit in the hole.'
>
> 'Yeah, Satch,' I said. 'But not by much. I'll bet you a fifth of Old Forester that you can't throw it through there.'
>
> 'Wild Child,' he said, 'I'll see you tomorrow night.'
>
> So the next night Satch showed up for batting practice—first time in his life he'd ever been early. I took a few baseballs, went out to the outfield, and stepped off about 60 feet 6 inches, the distance to the mound from home. Satch ambled out, took the ball, brought it up to his eye like he was aiming it, and let fire.
>
> I couldn't believe it. The ball hit the hole, rattled around, and dropped back out. He'd come that close, but I figured it was his best shot.

Satch took another ball and drilled the hole dead center. The ball went right through, and I haven't seen it since.

'Thank you, Wild Child,' Satch said, and then went back into the clubhouse.

When The Master pitched his last major league game in 1965 for Kansas City, the lights went out after his three-inning stint and 9,000 matches were lighted. The crowd then sang good-by to Satchel with "Rockin' Chair," "Silver Threads Among the Gold," and "The Old Gray Mare."

Satchel even appeared in a motion picture, *The Wonderful Country,* in 1957. The movie starred Robert Mitchum and Julie London. Paige later commented, "Except for learning to ride the horse, doing that movie wasn't too hard. I've been in show business most of my life ya know."

Satchel did promotional work for several minor league clubs during the 1970s, but as he moved into the 1980s, his health deteriorated from emphysema and heart disease. On 1981, he made one of his last public appearances at the Negro League Reunion in Ashland, Kentucky. While visibly ill, The Master's speech let everyone know that he had lost neither his humor nor his spirit.

"I'm glad to be here," he said, "At my age, I'm glad to be anywhere."

"You know," he continued, "when I told them in Cooperstown that we had men who didn't have to go to their farm clubs to play in the majors, they got mad and told me to sit down. That's the reason I don't go back to Cooperstown. Two of the men I was talkin' about are sittin' right here beside me, Monte Irvin and Willie Mays."

As his health worsened, Satchel's second wife, Lahoma, suffered with him. A beautiful woman, with a smile bright enough to light up the universe, she cared for him to the very end on June 8, 1982.

Sixteen young members of the Kansas City Bluejays baseball team pressed their caps to their chests and stood in reverent silence as the black 1938 Packard hearse carried The Master to his island in Forest Hill Memorial Park Cemetery in Kansas City, Missouri. Later, they listened to Reverend Cleavor, the family pastor:

If we listen very careful, we can hear Satchel say, 'I have fought a good fight, I kept the faith, and I've finished the race.'

Don't be sad, because Satchel Paige pitched a complete inning.

Josh

Josh Gibson, Jr. and his family, along with his father's sister, Annie, journeyed to Cooperstown in August of 1972 to accept the Hall of Fame's posthumous tribute to the great slugger. Even as his fame spread, however, Josh still rested in the obscure and neglected grave in Allegheny Cemetery on Tenth Avenue in Pittsburgh.

Then in July of 1974, Pedro Zorilla came up from Puerto Rico for the major league All-Star game at Pittsburgh's Three Rivers Stadium. Zorilla, a long-time promoter of Puerto Rican baseball and once owner of the Santurce club, idolized Josh Gibson and wanted to visit his grave. He contacted Ted Page.

Ted remembered the time well. "Pete and I went out to Allegheny Cemetery, but we couldn't find the marker. There were these little round metal caps all over, most of them overgrown with grass and weeds. We finally realized that we would have to get a number before we could find where Josh was buried. We got hold of the undertaker who'd handled Josh's funeral and he came out to the cemetery with us and helped us to locate the grave.

"I was embarrassed about the grave. I knew I should have done something about it long ago. I decided to raise some money to give Josh a proper stone. I asked Willie Stargell for some money. He really cared about the guys who played in Negro baseball and he was especially interested in Josh, a big slugger like himself. Willie gave me $100 and promised to give me more if I needed it.

"As it turned out, I gave Stargell his money back because the baseball commissioner's office found out about the situation and put up all the money for the gravestone. It wasn't a fancy marker, but it did say that Josh was a great Negro league ballplayer for the Crawfords and the Homestead Grays. I sure felt better after they put it up. Josh deserved it. He was one of the very best."

Cool

During the winter of 1952, with the black leagues agonizing in their death throes, Cool Papa returned to St. Louis in search of more reliable employment. He became a night watchman at St. Louis City Hall and also scouted for the old St. Louis Browns until the team left the city for Baltimore in 1954. The Browns even offered him a $10,000 contract to play for them in 1953. "Sure I can hit," he told

Cool Papa Bell and Judy Johnson at
Cooperstown in 1975 for Johnson's Hall of
Fame induction.

Bill Veeck, "but I'm too old. My legs are gone. I can't catch the ball the other
guy hits. I'm not going to make a fool of myself. Pride is more important than
money."

Bell settled into a life of virtual obscurity, never dreaming he would receive
any special recognition for his baseball brilliance. Then came the Ted Williams
speech, the Negro League Committee, and on February 13, 1974, the joyous news
of his election to the Hall of Fame. In Cooperstown that July, he sat in the bright
sunshine with his fellow inductees, Mickey Mantle, Whitey Ford, Jocko Conlan,
and Mrs. Jim Bottomley, who accepted for her deceased husband. Cool Papa,
striking in a white suit, thanked everyone for allowing him "to smell the rose"
while he was still alive.

Selection to the Hall of Fame resulted in increased publicity for the man with
flying feet. Articles about his baseball exploits have appeared in *American Heritage,
St. Louis Magazine, Baseball History, The Sporting News, Sports History,* and soon,

Highlights for Children. Senator Thomas Eagleton honored him in the *Congressional Record.* On Papa Bell's wall hangs a letter from President Ronald Reagan commending him for his accomplishments. The city of St. Louis even changed the name of his home street from Dickson to "James Cool Papa Bell Avenue."

The increased publicity has led to increased responsibilities. Signing autographs stands foremost among these responsibilities in Bell's mind. "The fans are the most important part of our game," he says. "I will sign everything I can for as long as I can."

The volume of Cool's mail has grown quite substantially over the years. Now, having lost one eye to glaucoma, and losing sight in the other, autographing has become very difficult and painstaking for him. Still, on good days, he does his best to sign the many requests.

Bell also feels that he has a serious responsibility to the Hall of Fame. "When a man is elected to the Hall of Fame, I think he should go up to Cooperstown every year for the induction ceremonies. I don't agree with these guys who go up there when they're enshrined, and then you never see them again. Look at Charley Gehringer. He's even a little older than I am and he's up there every year."

"I remember the time a few years ago when Enos Slaughter was enshrined. Near the end of his speech, he called Ted Williams up to the podium. Slaughter had been playing right field for the National League in the 1941 All-Star game when Williams won it for the American League with a home run. The ball had bounced back on the field and Slaughter saved it all those years. It sure was nice of him to give it to Williams."

True to his word, and despite increasingly poor health, Bell has never missed a trip to Cooperstown since his induction. Even in 1989, just a few days after undergoing minor surgery, he made the long journey from St. Louis. When asked about the dangers of such an experience for an ill 86-year-old man, he says, "So what if I died in Cooperstown. Baseball has been my life anyway."

Bell also continues to speak out on issues he considers important, one of which is baseball's treatment of Curt Flood. "Flood was a brave man and baseball treated him very poorly. It's because of him that these guys are makin' all the money now. They should give him some of their money."

Cool maintains close ties with the St. Louis Cardinals. Stan Musial, whose statue stands outside of Busch Memorial Stadium, has made sure all the doors have been open for him and that he has been treated with the utmost respect. Lou Brock, Ozzie Smith, Willie McGee, and Vince Coleman have all benefited from Cool's baseball wisdom.

While time has slowed Bell's flying feet, it has not dimmed his zest for life, his love for Clara (his wife of over 60 years), or for his devotion to baseball. He's still a real Cool Papa.

Charley

After Oscar Charleston finished his career as manager of the Indianapolis Clowns, he spent several winter seasons barnstorming with Satchel Paige. The two had never been close because of conflicting personalities. While Paige was fun-loving and unpredictable, Charleston was the stern, disciplined company man.

Still, the two men respected each other's talent, competitive fire, and unrelenting defiance of racism. Because of this respect, Satchel provided some paydays for the needy Charleston.

In 1949, Charley began working in the baggage department of Philadelphia's Pennsylvania Railroad Station. Some of the old-timers knew of his baseball exploits, but the youngsters laughed at his stories and he became an object of ridicule as the typical old man who fantasized about his athletic past.

Charleston died of a heart attack on October 5, 1954. The funeral took place in Philadelphia and burial was at home in Indianapolis. In 1976, his sister journeyed to Cooperstown to accept a Hall of Fame plaque for the man who may have been the greatest baseball player ever.

Judy

Following his retirement, Judy scouted for both the Philadelphia Athletics and the Philadelphia Phillies. He also became the first black coach in the major leagues, serving on the staff of Manager Eddie Joost of the Philadelphia Athletics in 1954.

During his acceptance speech at Cooperstown in 1975, Judy's emotions overcame him. As the tears flowed, his son-in-law Billy Bruton, a former Milwaukee Brave and Detroit Tiger center fielder, came up on the platform to reassure him. Judy regained his composure, returned to the microphone, and finished his speech with words that caused tears to form in the eyes of many people in the audience. Perhaps speaking for all the old black stars elected to the Hall, as well as for himself, he said simply, "I am so grateful."

Judy was deeply moved again when the city of Wilmington, Delaware renamed the park where he had played as a boy as Judy Johnson Park. Mr. Sunshine died in 1989, a beautiful serene man who represented the very best of black baseball.

Crutch

Jimmie Crutchfield, a superb player, was perhaps the most underrated of the Crawfords. He could do it all, with the bat, on the bases, and in the field. He finished his career with the Cleveland Buckeyes in 1945 and returned to Chicago where he had played for the American Giants in several of his later seasons. He worked for the Chicago post office for twenty-five years and then spent three more years as a bank messenger before retiring.

Although 79 years old, he gives the impression of a man of 60, with his flashing eyes and a strong handshake. He is quite articulate, with his sharp mind and his incredible memory.

"Who hit the ball you caught in the 1934 East-West game to start a game-ending double play?" The reply comes quickly, "Red Parnell of the Nashville Elite Giants."

"Who did you throw out at the plate?" "Mule Suttles of the Chicago American Giants. And Bill Perkins of the Crawfords was the catcher. Josh had moved to the outfield."

"Who hit the ball on which you made the great barehanded catch in the 1935 game?" "Biz Mackey of the Philadelphia Stars."

The precision extends to the wonderful scrapbooks Jimmie has maintained over the years, which details his career as far back as his first game with Satchel Paige in 1930 while playing for the Birmingham Black Barons. When the scrapbooks open, the air fills with memories. They are proud memories for Jimmy Crutchfield. After all, he was one of the best on what may have been the greatest team of all time.

Ted

Shortened by a knee injury, Ted Page's career ended with the Baltimore Black Sox in 1937. Ted earned a fine living for himself and his lovely wife, Juanita, by becoming proprietor of a prosperous bowling alley in Pittsburgh and by doing public relations work for the Gulf Oil Company.

Ted remained very close to baseball over the years. He became a regular in the Pittsburgh Pirates clubhouse and was befriended by Roberto Clemente, Manny Sanguillen, and especially, by Willie Stargell. From Ted, they learned about their rich baseball heritage.

Ted Page understood the heritage well. He relished his status as a member of the Crawfords' legendary outfield—Bell, Crutchfield, and Page. Despite the legendary status, Page was not a great ball player, but rather a very good one. He could hit, and he had wonderful speed, but his defensive abilities were mediocre at best. Actually, the Crawfords improved when Sammy Bankhead replaced Page in the outfield.

When the doors of the Hall of Fame opened to Negro league players, many names surfaced as possible enshrinees. One of those names was Ted Page. He traveled to Cooperstown every summer for the induction ceremonies, hoping, it seemed, to gain the recognition he needed for election. He was a legend and an articulate man who carried himself with great dignity, but these factors were not enough to overcome his lack of greatness on the field.

Following Juanita's death in 1984, Ted pulled a troubled young man off the streets of Pittsburgh and tried to turn his life around. In the fall of 1985, Ted returned home one afternoon and found the young man robbing his house. Ted confronted him and was beaten to death. It was a tragic ending for such a strong, genuine man.

Bankhead

Sam Bankhead, the Crawford's brilliant "do-everything" player, was an intelligent baseball man who ended his Negro League career in 1950 as player-manager of the Homestead Grays. He became very much a father figure to Josh Gibson, Jr., an infielder with the Grays during the 1949 and 1950 seasons.

The Grays folded in 1950, and the Pittsburgh Pirates signed Bankhead to manage their farm club in Farnham, Quebec. The Pirates also signed Josh, Jr., and he played second base for Farnham until a severe foot injury ended his career. Bankhead managed Farnham until 1952 when the Pirates asked him to take a cut in pay. At the age of 42, he decided to quit baseball for good. He returned to Pittsburgh and worked as a common laborer for many years.

Tragedy struck the Bankhead family in 1976. In May, Sam lost his brother Dan to throat cancer. Dan pitched three seasons with the Brooklyn Dodgers. Just two months later, his brother Fred, for many years an infielder with the Memphis Red Sox, died in an automobile accident. Then, on Saturday night, July 24, Sammy became involved in an argument with a fellow employee at the William Penn Hotel in downtown Pittsburgh. When Bankhead turned his back to walk away, the other man pulled a small handgun and shot him in the back of the head, killing him instantly.

How exciting it must have been for those fans who sat in the stands at Greenlee Field on a warm yesteryear afternoon, feeling the sun on their faces, smelling the new-mown grass, and watching the Pittsburgh Crawfords weave their magic. Perhaps, if only for a few moments, the pop of Satchel's fastball, the crack of Josh's bat, and Cool Papa's flying feet allowed them to flee the dismal times of Depression America. Perhaps, too, for the black fans, the exploits of the men on the field aroused a sense of pride in their race that allowed them to escape the evils of racism which surrounded them.

Those Pittsburgh Crawford fans saw a group of confident, talented men who bowed to no baseball team on Earth. They blended talent and teamwork to form one of the most awesome baseball machines in history.

Remember the Pittsburgh Crawfords, black baseball's most exciting team. They loved to play baseball, and they played it very well.

Appendix
The Matchup

---

*If I had been pitching to people like Babe Ruth and
Lou Gehrig they would have hit fewer homers and
those lifetime batting averages might not be so
impressive.*

Satchel Paige, 1979
Springfield, Illinois

---

*T*he reason most often given for excluding pre-Jackie Robinson black players from all-time best teams and lists of all-time best players is the lack of statistics. Granted, we have little statistical evidence to verify their greatness. More concerned with sheer survival, the black teams and their players placed little emphasis on numbers. As Cool Papa Bell says,"Many times they didn't even keep the book during the game," and much of what was recorded has not survived the ravages of time.

Satchel Paige suggested that his presence in the American League during his prime might have had a significant effect on statistics. Perhaps he was right. After all, in Satchel's era, and that of Ruth and Gehrig, each league had only eight teams and they played a 154-game schedule. The teams played each other 22 times every year. Ruth and Gehrig might well have batted against Paige some 20 or more times a season. The Master certainly would have had an impact.

Satchel, with his big ego, tended to overlook the effect of other black pitchers on the statistics of Ruth, Gehrig, and the other hitters. Satchel also failed to mention the impact that great black hitters, men such as Josh Gibson, Oscar Charleston, and Willie Wells, would have had on the American or National Leagues.

Black baseball is criticized because the competition was sometimes of minor league calibre. The criticism is valid because black teams normally played other black teams, rather than an integrated blend of black, brown, and white. The same criticism therefore holds true for big league teams because they normally played against only white competition, a talent pool diminished by the absence of colored players. The American and National Leagues had no just basis for calling themselves major leagues until integration, and the statistics compiled before then must be considered inflated by the reduced quality of competition.

We do have some statistical background for evaluating black players, and this background continues to grow. Still, the opinions of their contemporaries, both on the field and in the press box, remain the best indicators of their abilities.

By consensus, although certainly open to argument, the 1927 New York Yankees stand as the greatest white team of all time. The 1935 Pittsburgh Crawfords, again subject to argument, are the consensus choice as the best black team. Following is a position by position comparison of the two teams, going five deep into each of the pitching staffs. Since it is impossible to be statistically objective, for the reasons cited above, the comparisons are obviously subjective, based primarily on the observations of those who saw the men play.

Pitchers

Pittsburgh Crawfords/Satchel Paige(RH)

Paige, with overpowering stuff and exquisite control, ranks as one of the best of all time, a Hall-of-Famer in every sense of the word. He was also a good hitter for a pitcher and fielded his position quite well.

New York Yankees/Waite Hoyt(LH)

While also in the Hall of Fame, Hoyt is perhaps overrated. He was a good, but not great pitcher. He lacked Paige's overpowering stuff, although he too had fine control.

Advantage - Paige

*****

Pittsburgh Crawfords/Theolic Smith(RH)

They called Smith "Fireball" for good reason, as he had an outstanding fastball. He also featured a knuckleball and a superb change-up. He sometimes had control problems.

New York Yankees/Herb Pennock

Pennock also has a place in Cooperstown. A very intelligent man, he was adept at identifying hitter's weaknesses and then applying the observations to his pitching patterns.

Advantage - Pennock

*****

Pittsburgh Crawfords/Leroy Matlock(LH)

Matlock was a power pitcher with excellent control. Like Bob Gibson, he was absolutely fearless. Nobody could intimidate him.

New York Yankees/Urban Shocker(RH)

Shocker was a vastly underrated hurler with good stuff and good control. He may deserve Hall of Fame recognition more than Hoyt and Pennock.

Advantage - Even

*****

Pittsburgh Crawfords/Bertrum "Nat" Hunter(RH)

Hunter featured a good fastball and an outstanding curve. He sometimes lost his concentration, however.

New York Yankees/Bob Shawkey(RH)

Shawkey, like Shocker, should probably be rated at least as high as Hoyt and Pennock. By 1927, he was just about finished, but the veteran could still be counted on for a crafty performance from time to time.

Advantage - Shawkey

*****

Pittsburgh Crawfords/Sam Streeter(LH)

A spitball pitcher with splendid control, Streeter was in his final season in 1935. Like Shawkey, he could still be relied on, especially in clutch situations. Streeter most often worked in relief.

New York Yankees/Wilcey Moore(RH)

While Streeter had experience, Moore had youth. He had wonderful stuff, including a great sinking fastball. Moore was a relief pitcher.

Advantage - Even

*****

Catcher

Pittsburgh Crawfords/Josh Gibson

Hall-of-Famer Gibson ranks as one of the all-time great hitters both for average and power. He had fine running speed, and while he had an outstanding arm, he was only an average defensive catcher.

New York Yankees/Benny Bengough, Pat Collins, John Grabowski

These three shared the catching duties. All were only journeyman.

Advantage - Gibson

*****

First Base

Pittsburgh Crawfords/Oscar Charleston

Hall-of-Famer Charleston had slowed down appreciably by 1935. Still, he played fine defense, ran the bases with great intelligence, and hit when it really counted.

New York Yankees/Lou Gehrig

Gehrig, a future Hall-of-Famer, was just beginning to emerge as a superstar in 1927. He hit for average, hit the long ball, and drove in runs in bunches. He was an excellent base runner, but his first base play was still mediocre at that time.

Advantage - Gehrig

*****

The Pittsburgh Crawfords

Second Base

Pittsburgh Crawfords/Dick Seay

Dick Seay was a magnificent second baseman, incomparable at turning the double play. He was only an average hitter and had very poor foot speed.

New York Yankees/Tony Lazzeri

Lazzeri swung a big bat, ran well, and played a fine defensive second base.

Advantage - Lazzeri

*****

Third Base

Pittsburgh Crawfords/Judy Johnson

Johnson, another Hall-of-Famer, played the game with great intelligence. He could do it all — hit, run, throw, and field.

New York Yankees/Joe Dugan

Joe Dugan was a heady veteran who, like Johnson, could do everything. He ranks just a notch below Johnson.

Advantage - Johnson

*****

Shortstop

Pittsburgh Crawfords/Chester Williams

Williams was an excellent defensive shortstop, very steady in the field. He could run well, hit for average, and deliver good extra-base power.

New York Yankees/Mark Koenig

While Mark Koenig possessed similar abilities to Williams, he had more raw talent. He tended to be very inconsistent and sometimes erratic.

Advantage - Even

*****

Left Field

Pittsburgh Crawfords/Jimmie Crutchfield

Crutchfield hit well, ran well, and played absolutely brilliant defense.

New York Yankees/Bob Meusel

Meusel was a splendid hitter for power, average, and production. He had an enormous throwing arm, but very limited defensive range. His effort was sometimes questionable.

Advantage - Even

*****

160

Appendix

Center Field

Pittsburgh Crawfords/Cool Papa Bell

An excellent lead off man, Hall-of-Famer Bell swung a potent bat. The fastest man every to play baseball, he ranks as perhaps the game's best defensive center fielder.

New York Yankees/Earl Coombs

Like Bell, a fine lead off man, Coombs also featured speed, line-drive hitting, and outstanding defense. He falls short of Bell, however.

Advantage - Bell

*****

Right Field

Pittsburgh Crawfords/Sam Bankhead

Bankhead could hit, run, and play the outfield with the best. His arm compared with those of Martin Dihigo and Roberto Clemente.

New York Yankees/Babe Ruth

Hall-of-Famer Ruth remains incomparable.

Advantage - Ruth

*****

Who would win a series between these two great clubs? Create your own field of dreams and decide for yourself. Here are your batting orders:

Pittsburgh Crawfords	*New York Yankees*
Bell, CF	Coombs, CF
Crutchfield, LF	Koenig, SS
Charleston, 1B	Ruth, RF
Gibson, C	Gehrig, 1B
Johnson, 3B	Meusel, LF
Bankhead, RF	Lazzeri, 2B
Williams, SS	Dugan, 3B
Seay, 2B	Bengough, C
Paige, P	Hoyt, P

For Further Information

Film

Davidson, Craig/Producer. *There Was Always Sun Shining Someplace.* Refocus Productions, 1983.

Literature

Holway, John B. *Voices From the Great Black Baseball Leagues.* Dodd Mead, 1975.

Holway, John B. *Blackball Stars: Negro League Pioneers.* Meckler Books, 1988.

Peterson, Robert. *Only the Ball Was White.* Prentice-Hall, 1970.

Rogosin, Donn. *Invisible Men: Life in Baseball's Negro Leagues.* Atheneum, 1983.

Photograph Credits

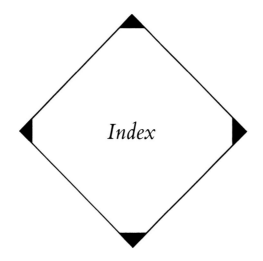

Index

More Baseball Books to Order from
Wm. C. Brown's Line Up Are:

☐ **THE LAST .400 HITTER**
by John B. Holway

1991/304 pages/Cloth/ISBN 14129/$19.95

In the Summer of 1941 Ted Williams and Joe DiMaggio stood at the most dramatic peaks of their lives. DiMaggio created a legend in the best two months he ever played. Williams reached a height that no other man has scaled in 60 years. John B. Holway tells us the story about the famous last .400 hitter—Ted Williams.

☐ **THE GREATEST CATCHERS OF ALL TIME**
by Don Honig

1991/160 pages/Cloth/ISBN 12806/$18.95

A one-of-a-kind book—a one-of-a-kind series. In this unique book, Donald Honig highlights the careers of the 15 greatest catchers of all time.

☐ **THE PITTSBURGH CRAWFORDS: Memories of Black Baseball's Most Exciting Team**
by Jim Bankes

1991/195 pages/Paper/ISBN 12889/$15.95

A tribute to the most talented team in the National Negro League during the '30s: the Pittsburgh Crawfords.

☐ **BASEBALL BY THE BOOKS**
by Andy McCue

1990/175 pages/Paper/ISBN 12764/$14.95

If you love baseball and love reading about it even more, this book is a must for you! For over three years, Andy McCue has researched, gathered, and compiled over 1,300 entries in his new baseball fiction bibliography.

☐ **TEACHING THE MENTAL ASPECTS OF BASEBALL: A Coach's Handbook**
by Al Figone, Humboldt State University

1990/240 pages/Paper/ISBN 12767/$15.95

At last! A practical book for coaches and players of all levels about integrating the mental aspects of baseball when executing the technical skills.

☐ **BUILDING A BETTER HITTER**

by Stephen Pecci; Foreword by George Foster

1990/112 pages/Paper/ISBN 11404/$10.95

There's more to successful hitting than just good swings. Pecci's new book provides coaches and players with a program that produces better hitters.

☐ **THE COMPLETE BASEBALL HANDBOOK: Strategies and Techniques for Winning**

by Walter Alston and Don Weiskopf

1984/530 pages/Cloth/ISBN 6819/$19.95

Drawing upon 23 years of experience as manager of the Brooklyn/L.A. Dodgers—seven league pennants, and four World Series Championships—the late Walter Alston's time-honored philosophy on both the basics and fine points of coaching is geared toward producing better ball players and winning teams!

ORDER FORM

TO ORDER ANY OR ALL OF THESE TITLES:

1. **CALL Toll Free 1–800–338–5578**

2. Send check or money order plus appropriate state tax and $1.00 shipping and handling for each book ordered along with a list of the books you would like to receive (include ISBN numbers) to:

Wm. C. Brown Publishers
2460 Kerper Boulevard
Dubuque, Iowa 52001

SHIP TO: _____ Book Total $ _____

_____ Tax $ _____

City _____ State _____ Zip _____ Shipping $ _____

Total $ _____

REMEMBER TO ASK FOR A **FREE** SPORTS PAGE CATALOG
LISTING ALL OF OUR TITLES